Bobby Ochs, Kid FROM THE Bronx AND Restaurant Partner TO THE Stars

FROM KASHE VARNISHKES TO CAVIAR TO HUMBLE PIE

A Memoir by

BOBBY OCHS

NEWMAN SPRINGS PUBLISHING
320 Broad Street
Red Bank, NJ 07701

First originally published by Newman Springs Publishing 2022

Pictured with Bobby on the cover: Patrick Swayze,
Britney Spears, Marla Maples, and Ashford & Simpson

ISBN 978-1-68498-517-3 (Paperback)
ISBN 978-1-68498-518-0 (Digital)

Printed in the United States of America

To my beautiful wife Carolyn (who stayed with me through thick and thin), my daughter Samantha, my sisters Florence and Genie, my brother Lenny, my Mother and Father.—and anyone who ate and had a drink at any of my restaurants.

Acknowledgments

I would like to give a big thanks to Arlene Kayatt my collaborator and editor, without her literary contribution, I would still be working to figuring out how to complete this book.

I would also like to give thanks to my nephew Prof. Edward B. Burger, for his support and generosity in helping get this book to the finish line.

Advance Praise

"Bobby Ochs, a kid from the Bronx, had a talent for collecting celebrities like some of us collected stamps. Combined with his love of restaurants, he became a pioneer in the slam-bang, razzle-dazzle world of NY's post-1960s bar and restaurant scene. A wow and fascinating journey."

—Silas Seandel, Army buddy & lifelong friend

"To some, he's a brilliant restaurateur, to others he's a daring risk-taker, still others see him as a creative raconteur who collaborated with some of the biggest celebrities from the '80s, '90s, and '00s. But to me, I only knew him as 'Uncle Robbie'—my mother's brother. So, reading about his many adventures not only was engrossing and entertaining, but also offered the lessons of life one would expect from a family member. Even if you are not related to Bobby, you will enjoy his stories and take his life lessons to heart."

—Edward B. Burger, Ph.D., mathematics video semi-celebrity

"I have had the privilege of knowing Bobby for nearly fifty years. During the '70s–'80s Bobby was a visionary as to what was new and cutting edge. His restaurants were always top shelf and special. My wife Ann and I shared many fun and exciting times at Bobby's restaurants which I will never forget."

—Alan Obsatz, owner of Butterfield Market

"I have known Bobby as a friend and past neighbor. I have heard his life story and I told him it would make a fantastic book and movie. After 41 years in law enforcement 30 of which 1 was a federal agent his story and career was remarkable! The best of luck this book will be a must read!"

—Paul Miller, retired FBI agent

Contents

A "What If…"

I wonder how much money I could get on eBay or from some private collector's Bitcoins if I still had the denture impression of Leon Trotsky's mouth today. For several months in 1917, over a hundred years ago, Leon Trotsky lived in the Bronx for three months with his wife and kids, long enough for my dad, a twenty-two-year-old dental mechanic, to make Trotsky's new dentures—my dad's claim to fame. Trotsky left for Russia in May 1917 and, by the end of the year, was second only to Lenin in the Bolshevik party and chomping his meals with my dad's dentures.

In 1936, with the assistance of Mexican artist Diego Rivera, Trotsky sought asylum in Mexico and was assassinated there in 1940, with my dad's dentures going down with him. While my father was a quiet and unassuming man, he took pride in having made the Bolshevik's teeth, and he seemed to enjoy the touch of celebrity, which he definitely passed along to me. And here's the rest of the story…

Adolf and Minnie Come to America

M y parents were born in Poland but met and married in America. They each came to America in the early twentieth century, both immigrants from Poland. My father was born in 1895, my mother in 1900. They came at different times. He was Adolf (spelled with an *f* and became *Adolph* when he came to America) Ochs; she was Minnie Schwartz. I came across a letter after my father died from a woman my mother had written to while she was still in Poland, telling the woman that she would be living and working in New York and wanted to meet an eligible man. While my parents met and married in America, I don't know if the introduction was by the Dolly ("Hello, Dolly") Levi matchmaker my mother reached out to.

These musings swirl through my mind as I'm nearing the eighth decade of my life (easier to say than I'm closing in on next year) and want to share the stories I have to tell growing up in the Bronx of the '40s and '50s and how having dreams and making them happen is what life's about. I'd like my daughter Samantha to understand her father, to know that he lived his life true to his belief that taking risks, following your heart and dreams, and not giving up is what life's about and that win or lose, you go for it. Giving up is not an option. If you fall down, you get up. Not getting up is the failure.

I was the youngest of four children. Actually, I was my parents' fifth child. Their two-year-old son Ted died two years before I was born, and the family whisper was that I was born to replace him. What, if anything, that whisper has had on my life, I don't know, and I'm not looking into it. Being the youngest child in the Ochs family meant that my oldest sister, Florence, was thirteen when I was born and that the adults in my family were much older than I was.

Unfortunately, in the life cycle, that exposed me to too many deaths as I was growing up. The earliest and hardest for me was one I couldn't really fathom: my mother dying when I was seven. I was told when she went to the hospital that something was wrong with her finger. After she died, I wouldn't let anyone touch my fingers.

As a seven-year-old, I was left pretty much on my own. My father would leave every morning to his office. My sisters, who were thirteen years and ten years older, and my brother Lenny, who was six years older than me, would leave in the morning to go off to high school or college. I would go off by myself to elementary school PS 53. My father would give me a couple of bucks to eat lunch. I was pretty much on my own.

At the age of thirteen, I found College Rec Pool Room, which was located in the basement of a building on 170th Street. It was across the street from Taft High School and next door to the Elsmere Catering and Wedding Hall, causing couples in tuxes and gowns to collide with guys with pool cues. For years, I spent more time in the poolroom than in the schoolroom.

One night, at the age of fifteen, I was returning home after a tough night in the poolroom. I lost a lot but not as much of a loss as I soon found out. It was about midnight when I got home. My father was sleeping. Florence and Lenny were not home, and Genie had recently gone to California and was on her way back to New York. The phone rang. I answered. The voice on the phone said, "I am Officer So and So from the Oklahoma Highway Patrol. Do you know a Eugenia Ochs?"

"Yes," I said, "She's my sister."

The officer replied matter-of-factly, "Your sister was in a car crash and was killed. What would you like us to do with the body?"

I was fifteen at the time, and the loss of Genie was devastating. Genie, who taught me to read before I was of school age. Genie, who taught me how to read the box score of the Yankees games; to this day, I still check the box scores. Genie, when it was time for her to go to high school, was one of the first girls to pass the test to be accepted

3

to the all-boys Bronx High School of Science, which was very difficult to get into. She rejected their offer. Actually, she didn't want to go to any school. While attending Long Island University, she enrolled in drama studies and moved to Greenwich Village, which was unusual at the time for a young girl to be so independent.

After college, she lived on her own in Miami. Not only did Genie teach me to read, she also showed me the joy of theater and the arts. She shaped my thinking by watching her live her short life on her terms. She was twenty-five years old when she was killed.

The death of my father a year later blew me away. I found him in his bed when I came home in the late morning from a doctor's appointment because I hadn't been feeling well. I had left the house before he would have left for his office, which was always at eight in the morning. When I got home around eleven, his bedroom door was closed. I could tell that he was still home and uneasily opened the door. He was in bed. I knew, just knew…and walked over to him. His body was lifeless. I called the doctor I had just left and told him.

In some ways, his death, if not expected, was inevitable. Although in good health for a potbellied, sixty-three-year-old smoker, he died a week before the one-year anniversary of Genie's death, and we would be going to the cemetery for her unveiling, the marking of the deceased with a gravestone, an ancient Jewish custom when mourners and their family gather at the graveside for a ritual unveiling. Genie's death was one too many for my father, whose parents, siblings, and other family members were massacred in a pogrom in Poland, and whose third child, a son, died at two, and whose wife died of breast cancer when she was forty-nine.

The Ochs Family of Teller Avenue

My sisters Florence and Genie, my brother Lenny, and I were first-generation Americans. Florence was thirteen when I came along in 1942, Genie was ten, Lenny was six. Several years before I was born, another child, Ted, died when he was two. By the time I was born, some thirty years after my mother and father arrived in America, we lived on Teller Avenue in the Bronx. If anyone asked someone living on Teller Avenue where they lived, they said, "Just off the [Grand] Concourse," which meant you hadn't yet arrived but were moving on up. In those years, the Grand Concourse was thought of as the Champs-Élysées of the Bronx, the epitome of status for those living in the Bronx. And if you actually lived on the Grand Concourse, well, that was big.

The Ochs family lived about five blocks east of the Concourse, and living in the East Bronx was definitely déclassé. The West Bronx, which had more cachet, started west of Jerome Avenue, where the overhead El-Train Track still stands. Teller Avenue was known to be more West Bronx than East Bronx, or so I choose to believe. A big plus for my Teller Avenue apartment building was its proximity to Yankee Stadium. It was more than ten blocks away and farther east, but from the five-story tenement rooftop (known as Tar Beach), you could hear the roar of the stadium crowd and see the stadium lights on game nights.

At 1345 Teller Avenue, we lived in a five-story walk-up in a cramped two-bedroom, one-bathroom apartment. In the hallways, exposed light bulbs hung from extended wires—same in our apartment. I guess my father had his own vision of what one needed for

5

comfort after growing up in an orphanage. I never learned very much about my mother's life before she came to America. While my father rarely spoke about his life in Poland, I learned from letters I found after he died in 1959 that he had carried on a lifelong correspondence with surviving members of his family, some of whom lived in the orphanage after he came to America. The letters told of deplorable conditions, their need for money, their wanting to come to America. In some letters, they would acknowledge the money my father sent them and detail the problems they were having in being able to use the money.

Our Teller Avenue neighborhood was generally working-class, as was most of the surrounding neighborhood. Fathers were laborers, salespeople, furriers, seltzer men, small business owners. Most mothers didn't work, and if they did, they were frowned upon, and their school-age kids were labeled as latchkey kids because their mother wasn't home when they got home after school.

Most parents in that part of the Bronx generally were not educated beyond high school, but education was the highest priority for their children. Their sons and daughters, they would make sure would be professionals: doctors, lawyers, teachers. While my sisters went to college, my brother and I didn't. The social strata in the east and west of the Bronx was pretty much the same. However, the West Bronx was thought to be a little higher on the socioeconomic and education scale. Those who lived in West Bronx tended to be teachers and accountants.

Most families in both parts of the Bronx were Jewish or Italian or Irish with a smattering of other Eastern European immigrants. Hispanics and Blacks and Asians were in the minority, and there were few enough that the entire neighborhood knew who they were. Brenda was the Black girl, Mabel the Chinese girl, Julio the Spanish boy. What was unspoken but tacitly understood was that you didn't marry outside your religion. There were sorry stories, all true, of Jewish families sitting shiva for a Jewish son or daughter who married a shiksa or a sheigetz, a non-Jewish boy or girl. The message was clear: no goyim in this family. Interracial marriages, for whatever reason, were not on the radar. If it happened or was discussed, I didn't know about it.

Mother Minnie

My mother's family, the Schwartzes, came to America in two stages. Grandpa and two of the children came first. Grandma and the two younger children followed several years later. My mother was the youngest. All of the Schwartzes who came to America settled in Brooklyn, where their children—my aunts, uncles, cousins—grew up. My mother's mother, who was known as the Bubba, lived with my family after Grandpa died and until shortly after I was born. Then she went to live with Aunt Faygeh, my mother's sister. After that—Grandma outlived my mother—she lived with her other children. My mother's sisters and brother remained in Brooklyn until death did they part. Their children generally lived nearby.

The Ochses and Schwartzes were tightly knit families, and in every way, my birth was the quintessential family event. My cousin Jack Golliger—make that Jack Golliger, MD—literally had the task of bringing me into the world, and it was a carefully crafted event. Uncle Adolph and Aunt Minnie would travel from the Bronx to Brooklyn, where their nephew Jack had hospital privileges and where Aunt Minnie's baby would be born.

Mind you, this is not the first time that Cousin Jack (or Dr. Jack, as he was known in the family) had a role in the medical affairs and treatment of other Ochs family members. When my twelve-year-old sister Florence had to have her tonsils removed, the procedure fell to Cousin Jack. He traveled to Aunt Minnie's Bronx apartment from Brooklyn, scalpel and satchel in tow, to remove Florence's tonsils but only after Florence climbed onto the kitchen table so the deed could be done. While it was an unlikely setting for a medical procedure and an unlikely operation for the ob-gyn doctor who Jack was, it was family, and that's what mattered.

Same tradition resulted in my being named Robert, when two teenagers—my sister Florence and cousin Ethel—told my parents that the new baby, if it was a boy, had to be named Robert after the 1940s movie star heartthrob Robert Taylor. So defying the Jewish tradition of naming newborns after the dearly departed, I was named Robert. Interestingly and maybe fortuitously, Robert Taylor played Johnny Eager, a gambling man in the film named *Johnny Eager*.

In looking back, and not for nothing, I'm seeing a road map, a pattern of celebrity emerging for that kid named Robert and sometimes Robbie when growing up. My ninety-something sister Florence always called me Robbie. Before that came my father's celebrity in making Trotsky's teeth. And throughout my life, I've been associated with celebrity, most famously as a partner to celebrities in the restaurant business, beginning with Ashford & Simpson at Twenty-Twenty and then with Patrick Swayze at Mulholland Drive Café, one of the hottest restaurants in the '90s. After that came a partnership with Marla Maples at Peaches and then Britney Spears at Nyla.

Adolf in Poland

My father wasn't much for talking about his life in Poland, except for saying that after his parents were murdered in a massacre of Jews in Poland, he went to live in an orphanage when he was five years old and was brought up there at the turn of the century, where he was trained to be a dental mechanic.

He left the orphanage and Poland in 1912 when he turned seventeen. His training as a dental mechanic served him well in being able to come to America because although he was required to be sponsored by an American who would be responsible if he fell on bad times (or in legal vernacular, if he became a public charge), he would have to have a job once he got here. My father's American sponsor, I believe, was either an uncle or cousin of his who had emigrated to America and became a successful businessman.

A vice, maybe a passion, that my father took with him to America was his love of the racetrack. He loved watching the horses trot and handicapping the winners. He told me that his interest began when he was fourteen or fifteen, when he and another orphan boy would make their way out of the orphanage and over to the racetrack. When he talked about it, he would have a twinkle in his eye, a shot of whiskey in one hand, a cigarette in the other, and a smile on his face. Some of my fondest memories of my dad were the times he spent with me handicapping, kibitzing, and dining at Yonkers and Roosevelt racetracks.

The Immigrant Dream

I n America, my father apprenticed as a dental mechanic in a dentist's office. His primary mastery was making false teeth, which helped make him a celebrity. In 1917, at twenty-two, my father had been living and working in the Bronx for five years and had opened his own dental mechanic office.

A bachelor, he ate out regularly at Bronx restaurants, the Triangle Diner in particular. Food there was strictly Eastern European. My father would be sitting alone at a table near another regular, Leon Trotsky, who was also sitting alone and was visiting New York with his family. My father and Trotsky would speak across their separate tables. My father probably noticed his bad teeth, or Trotsky may have asked for a dentist after learning of my father's profession. In any event, Trotsky went to the dentist my dad recommended, and the dentist sent the impression of Trotsky's teeth to my father, who made the impression of the Bolshevik's false teeth.

Alas, my father's mechanical dentistry was lost to history when Trotsky, teeth intact, was murdered in 1940. And the impression of Trotsky's teeth was nowhere to be found when my father died. Alas, a lost inheritance but not my father's claim to fame.

About Adolph

Every day when I was a young boy I can remember my father leaving our apartment on Teller Avenue between 169th Street and 170th Street at seven in the morning. Dressed in a three-piece suit with a necktie and a gold pocket watch in his vest pocket, and the gold chain draped into his pant pocket he completed the picture with a hat that matched the color of his suit. He headed to his office, Cosmopolitan Dental, on 167th Street between River and Jerome Avenues in the Bronx.

His office was a short distance from our apartment and could easily be walked in less than twenty minutes, but my father would take a taxi to work. He didn't have to dress in suit and tie. He owned his own dental mechanic shop and sat at his workbench making false teeth for his clients who were dentists and didn't deal directly with the public. He could have dressed in jeans and a T-shirt, but he chose to wear smart-looking suits. Maybe it was a sign of the times, and that's how businessmen dressed in the 1940s and '50s. Or maybe it was a certain pride he took in himself. He sure looked good for a man with a potbelly.

The dental shop was located on the second floor of a two-story building. It had an extralong staircase to climb to get to his office. Once entering, there was a reception space with a large wooden desk that had a folding top that opened and closed. On the desk beside daily newspapers and racing forms was an old-style phone. Even back in the '40s, it was old, an antique even back then. By the way, there were also bills to be paid and invoices to be collected filed in the desk.

As a young boy, I spent a lot of time sitting at this desk waiting for my father to finish work. Beyond the reception area was a large room flanked by two smaller rooms. The large room housed three workbenches with various machines used to manufacture dentures, full upper and lowers, partial plates, and whatever. My father worked at this station, and depending how busy he was, the other stations were manned by one or two helpers. Today, they would be known as assistants. Whether his helpers were needed or not, they would hang around the office creating a clubhouse atmosphere. When they were not at their work station, the helpers would be handicapping the races at Belmont or Yonkers Raceway.

There was Farmer Red. I assumed he was born on a farm and had red hair—hence, the name Farmer Red. I'm not sure if the barn on the farm was factual or that he was so naive that he seemed to come off a farm was the reason for his handle.

Then here was Willie the Barber. I asked my father, "Did Willie really cut hair. If so, why was he working for you?"

My father laughed and said, "Willie is not a barber. We call him that because he's always getting into trouble with the wrong people and manages to escape unharmed—another close shave—so he's Willie the Barber."

Joe Weinberg was just Joe—no nickname. He'd just come and go.

The banter between these guys and my father when they were discussing teeth went like this: Farmer Red, while holding the racing form, would say to no one in particular, "Who do you like in the first at Belmont?

Willie would say, "I think the 2 horse has a good shot. I might use him in the double."

Joe would nod and say, "Sounds good."

Then my father would say, "The 2 horse has no shot at all. I like the 5 horse."

This would go on all day.

Then there was Bobby Bacon, who worked for my father. Bobby Bacon had a deformed left leg, and it was shorter than his right leg.

So when he walked, he had a major limp, so it seemed like he was running while dragging his left leg behind.

Bobby Bacon was considered to be mentally slow. He worked for my dad and made deliveries to the dentists' offices to pick up impressions of teeth and would bring them to my father. When the work was done, Bobby would bring the finished dentures back to the dentist. He would also run whatever errands my father needed. I remember my father giving Bobby money to take me to see the Yankees play on several occasions. Whatever perceived shortcomings Bobby Bacon had, he managed to buy the best seats with the money my dad gave him with enough for hot dogs, peanuts, and sodas.

I always had a good time with Bobby. He didn't participate with my dad's cronies handicapping horses. He didn't have an interest in betting and came from a very poor family, so whatever my father paid him, Bobby gave to his mother. My father told me that Bobby Bacon's mother once won a Cadillac at a church raffle and decided to keep it rather than sell the car for money they very much needed because they are so poor that whenever the car ran out of gas, they would have to leave it wherever they were.

In the Bronx neighborhood where we lived, everyone called my father Doctor Ochs. This honorary doctor's degree was bestowed upon him by our neighbors because he would, from time to time, help people who couldn't afford to see a dentist for their dentures. He would make their false teeth free of charge and bypass the dentist. I remember sitting in the office, watching my father take the impression of an old woman's mouth. Normally, the dentist would do that. The next day, the woman would come back, and my father would place a beautiful set of upper and lower dentures in her mouth. The woman was thrilled and asked, "How much I owe you?"

My dad, knowing she couldn't afford to pay anything, said, "There's no charge."

The woman insisted on paying something. My dad, not wanting to insult her dignity, said, "Okay, the price is one dollar," and the old woman proudly took out one dollar from her purse and thanked my father for doing a wonderful job.

13

The first time I went to the racetrack was with my father, I was either nine or ten years old. I sat waiting at his desk in his office for him to finish up. The gang—Farmer Red, Willie the Barber, Joe, my dad, and I—was going for dinner at the Hungarian restaurant and then driving to Yonkers Raceway in Farmer Red's car. This would be the first activity, other than going to a movie or restaurant with my father, that I would be going with the gang and my father.

It was exciting. I couldn't be more thrilled than to be sitting in a smoke-filled car and going to the track with my father. By the way, the whole gang were heavy smokers. My father smoked some crazy Turkish cigarette before switching to Lucky Strike and thinking it would be healthier. Some joke, but that was the '40s and '50s.

We get to the track. It's nighttime. I'm with my father and his crew. At the time, you had to be over eighteen years old to get into the track, and Joe and Willie had some concern about my age, but my father said not to worry. "He's getting in," and I did without a hitch. I don't know how my father got the tickets. I don't know if he knew someone or paid someone off. All I know I was sitting in grandstand seats, looking at the half-mile track, watching harness horses warming up by trotting around under the lights with men and adults all around me, smoking cigarettes and cigars. I still remember the smell of cigars at a racetrack. I felt like one of the guys for the first time.

My father bought me my own program to handicap each race and showed me how to read it and how to decide which horse to bet. Farmer Red actually asked me whom I liked in the first. My dad tells me that the first race and the second race could be bet as a daily double, that you have to win both races to collect. He says, "I'm going to play the double using the 1 horse in the first race and the 3 horse in the second race."

I asked him, "How did you come to that decision?" figuring that he would show me some mathematical calculation off the program to come to selecting the 1-3 combination for the daily double.

He simply said, "Choppy"—he nicknamed me Choppy (why, I don't know)—"you were born on the thirteenth, so 1-3 it is."

So much for handicapping by math.

He takes me to the betting window, gives me two bucks, and says, "That's for you to bet." He says to play the 1 horse to win in the first. The horse's name, Jack Flanagan, I remember to this day.

I say, "What about the daily double?"

He says, "Forget the double. It's a sucker's bet. Just play the 1 horse to win," and so I did.

I was so excited watching Jack Flanagan the 1 horse run around the track and win. I couldn't wait to collect the nine dollars it paid for a two-dollar bet. I couldn't wait to make my next bet on the next race. My dad did play the 1-3 double, and he won. At the end of the night, I had turned the two dollars my dad gave me into thirty dollars.

Winning thirty dollars for a ten-year-old back in 1952 was a big win, but it took second place to the actual betting and watching the race, which got my juices flowing. Before that night, I was never so excited about anything. A shot of adrenaline flew through my body every time I bet. Winning money was icing on the cake. Being with my father on that night made it all the more meaningful. That was my bar mitzvah, the night, at ten years old, I became a man.

No More Minnie

My mother was forty-nine when she died in 1949. I was seven and still in public school. My sisters were in college, my brother in high school. What to do with Bobby? Dad's solution was to hire a woman to look after me and see that I got off to school, or at least in time to get there. The woman would be there when I got home and would stay until my dad, brother, or sister got home.

To share the burden and to make sure I ate at home or had a hot meal, my father hired another woman to do the cooking and housekeeping. Apparently, his business was doing well, and he was scoring at the racetrack. He always had a pencil and a newspaper in his hands as he handicapped the day's races. One summer, I recall he hit a two-horse parlay that paid over five hundred bucks, and he used the money to send me to summer camp and to hire Rosina Pozo to look after me.

Rosina Pozo was a stout Black woman. I thought of her as being tall, but no, she was just big. While I can't picture my mother too well, I do recall that Rosina was stocky like my mother. The other woman he hired to do the housekeeping and cooking, I don't remember at all, except that she was a terrible cook. Florence tells me that one afternoon, when Rosina wasn't there, I was home alone with the woman who did the cooking. She was in the living room watching Bess Myerson on TV in *The Big Payoff*. She was smoking while my evening dinner was cooking on the stove or in the oven. I couldn't stand the smell of whatever it was she was making and didn't like that she was smoking. So I went to the kitchen phone and called my father to report that she wasn't working, the food smelled, and I wouldn't eat whatever she was making. Hearing this and fearful that she overheard what I was saying, my father rushed home and relieved the woman of her job.

From my father and maybe my sisters—definitely not my brother—I learned my way around the kitchen. Many times, I'd meet my father for dinner or eat out by myself or have dinner at the home of a neighbor or school friend. While my criticism of the cooking, smoking woman was legitimate, it's not that I was used to good cooking. My mother would make chicken soup for Friday night dinner. She'd boil a whole chicken with soup greens and vegetables and add farfel—little square noodles—to the soup. We would eat the noodle soup as a first course followed by the boiled chicken with its meat falling off the bone. The chicken was almost tasteless, so I'd flavor it up and practically drown it in ketchup.

Friday night dinners continued after my mother died with either my father or my sisters doing the cooking. As long as there was ketchup on the table, I'd eat. While there was no gourmet cooking in the Ochs household when I was growing up, I do remember my father's being creative with my breakfast. I was fussy about how my eggs were cooked, so in order to get me to eat scrambled eggs, he would add anchovies to the scrambled eggs. Why he thought I would eat little oil-soaked fish in my scrambled eggs when I wouldn't eat soft scrambled eggs, I don't know, but I am glad that I forced myself to try this strange concoction. I liked it, and I got to like the boiled potato and sour cream dinner he made once a week. Turns out, my father was a man of many tastes. One night, after a big win at the track, he served us beluga caviar and chopped hard-boiled eggs on Ritz Crackers.

Family Dinners

G rowing up in the Bronx, I always looked forward to holiday dinners with the family, especially Thanksgiving. On Thanksgiving,
our closest relatives, the Kronishes, would come from Brooklyn
to our apartment on Teller Avenue. There was Uncle Louie, Aunt
Rachael, and Cousins William, Harry, Ethel, Freddy and Ichie. My
father would make a twenty-five-pound turkey with all the fixings,
including a delicious stuffing that every one of the Kronish clan
loved, especially Aunt Rachael.

One year, Aunt Rachael asked my father for his stuffing recipe.
My father, realizing if she had the stuffing recipe, she would then
want to do next year's Thanksgiving, and that would be a hassle.
We would have to take the subway and schlep to Brooklyn. So my
father wrote the recipe, leaving out the key ingredient pork, which is
a no-no in a Jewish household. Sometime after my father gave Aunt
Rachael the recipe sans pork, she called my father, saying she made
the stuffing, and no one in her family cared for it. My father said he
didn't understand why but guaranteed that when they come to the
Bronx next Thanksgiving, everyone would love the stuffing. He was
right.

Starting when I was about eight and shortly after my mother
died, I did most of the household errands, including shopping. With
Rosina sometimes accompanying me, I'd do the food shopping with
a list from my father, sisters, and brother of what to buy. Of course,
I had my own list and would schmooze and kibitz with the local
shopkeepers. My father gave me instructions about where to shop—

no *big* places, only small businesses. That meant buying meat from Irving the butcher, a stocky man who always wore a bloodied apron and smoked a cigar. He did all the butchering, and when he wasn't doing that, he'd use a scrubbed-down butcher block to play pinochle with his cronies. No health police in those days. If anybody complained or said anything, it didn't matter. Irving would tell them to shop someplace else. He would never give up butchering or pinochle.

If my shoes needed a shoemaker, I went to the one down the street. If I was buying candy or newspapers, I'd go to Al Reisner's corner candy store, where I would buy the newspaper and large Hoffman cream sodas and then cash in the empty glass bottles and accumulate the coins I got for their deposit. In later years, I used the coins to play pool.

For fruits and vegetables, I'd go to the market on Morris Avenue and 170th Street, where I also bought milk, butter, and cheese. For dry goods, I went to Itzik the grocer. Itzik would add up all the items on a brown paper bag in pencil as he repeated the amount of each item in Yiddish. For lox, whitefish, and chubs, I went to Mr. Fox's appetizing store, where pickles and sour tomatoes were loaded into big wooden barrels. Mr. Fox made sure the lox was always sliced very thin. He was known by the slogan hanging proudly in the store's window: "Best Lox by Fox." He was right. It was the best.

The reason my father told me to shop at these local stores was because they were owned by or the workers were refugees who had numbers tattooed on their arms from their time in Nazi concentration camps.

Bobby's Early Eating Out

It was February 1950 when my mother died. I was seven years old. My two sisters Florence and Genie were considerably older than me, both attending Long Island University at the time. My brother Lenny was in high school and about to enlist in the army, leaving my father to watch over me. My father worked as a dental mechanic (technician, as referred to today) and had an office on 167th Street between Jerome and River Avenues. My father worked long hours, and I was basically left on my own.

As a fifth grader at PS 53, I couldn't stand the smell or the food in the school cafeteria and refused to eat that crap and didn't want to bring my lunch from home, so my father would give me a couple of bucks every day to go out and eat my lunch at a restaurant. This began my lifelong love of restaurants. There was a luncheonette one block from the school where I would go, and I'd sit at the counter by myself. Percy the counterman would make me an egg salad sandwich on toast with a delicious thick vanilla malted. I realized my father was right when he told me to always leave a good tip to ensure that Percy would take good care of me.

Some days, I would skip lunch and wait until 3:00 p.m. when school ended to treat myself to a corned beef sandwich on rye with french fried potatoes and a Dr. Brown's cream soda at Buchnoff & Schwartz Deli on 170th Street near the Luxor Movie Theater. There were days I would go to my father's office after school and wait until he would finish work. The two of us would go to Spiegel's Hungarian Restaurant one block from my father's office. We would have a bowl of Hungarian goulash. Sometimes we would have dinner there with a group of my father's friends. The goulash was always delicious but always a little better eating with my father and his cronies.

The Concourse Garden, a Chinese restaurant on 170th Street just west of the Concourse, was where I went for their combination number 1, chicken chow mein, fried rice, an egg roll, tea, and ice cream—all for 1.25 dollars. Every day for all my years growing up, I ate at least one meal, if not all my meals, at a restaurant. I guess that started me on the way to my life in the restaurant business.

The most vivid memory I have of my mother was when I was about five and in kindergarten. One day, she showed up in my class-room carrying large bags. I didn't know why she was there and wasn't happy that she came to my classroom. My teacher greeted her as she placed the bags on the teacher's desk. Together, they unpacked a huge cake, cookies, and treats. It was my birthday. I remember how proud and happy my mother was as they lit the candles and sang happy birthday. To think that two years later, she would be gone is beyond words.

Long Island University

I remember taking the subway to LIU in Brooklyn with my sister Genie, who was a student there. I might have been eight or nine years old. Genie took me around, introducing me to some of her classmates and teachers. After making the tour of LIU, Genie took me next door to the Brooklyn Paramount Theater to see a movie. After the movie, we went across the street to Junior's Restaurant and Bakery. We had dinner, and for dessert, we shared a piece of strawberry shortcake.

While I can't recall Genie's friends or teachers I met that day or the movie we saw or the dinner we ate at Junior's, I cannot forget the strawberry shortcake we shared. It seemed to be two feet high and six inches wide, with fresh whipped cream stacked high and covering a fluffy pound cake with fresh huge strawberries topping this gigantic masterpiece. I couldn't believe my eyes. After biting into it, the taste lived up to the visual work of art. That's when I learned you eat with your eyes. Presentation is key, something I never forgot when opening my restaurants.

Public School 53, the elementary school I went to until I was ten, was a short walk or run from home. I didn't like going to class and having to read and write. I didn't like sitting either, too much time in one place. I liked sports and playing hoops with my friend Richie. After school, Richie and I would make our way to the schoolyard at Taft High School or Claremont Park, each several blocks in different directions from where we lived.

And there was this six-foot-six-inch-tall twenty-year-old guy who was always willing to play with us. He was good, very good. And why'd he played with us? Because he was Richie's big brother Ed Roman, who was a star of the 1950s City College basketball team and is one of the celebrity encounters in my life. Ed made me a good schoolyard player. The news of his arrest and scandal was front-page news in every newspaper, ending his playing pro ball in the NBA. The Roman family was devastated.

My father Adolph

Adolf and friend with horse, circa 1915

Adolf Ochs, circa 1917

Adolph Ochs, Minnie Ochs,
Eugenia Ochs, Florence Ochs,
Bronx, NY, circa 1935

My sister Genie & me, circa 1950

25

Bobby Ochs, six months old, Bronx, NY, 1942

Bobby Ochs, Teller Ave.,
Bronx, NY circa 1949

Bobby Ochs, Teller Ave.,
Bronx, NY circa 1949

What Could Have Been

With my background and challenges, it would have been easy to write me off. My mother died. My sisters were in college. My brother was in high school. My father worked. But I was a resilient, resourceful, easygoing kid, tall and thin and probably looked a little older than I was. However it happened, at thirteen, I ambled into the College Rec Pool Room, a local hangout for pool players and gamblers, located a few blocks from where I lived.

You had to be eighteen to get in. It said so right on the door in the entranceway. Made no difference. In I walked, chatted up a guy holding a pool stick, and became a pool player. For some reason, and I've never known why, Izzy Snow, who owned the place, let me stay and play. Must have sensed a kindred spirit.

And it was at the College Rec Pool Room that I hooked up with another kindred spirit, Milty Cohen. Although Milty was also underage at fourteen, he was accompanied by his father Chink Cohen. Chink ran the numbers operations in Manhattan and the Bronx. Chink was the man. What Chink said was gospel. So Milty, in his signature camel hair coat (a luxury unknown to me), and I became BFFs.

When I first saw Milty, I was surprised to see another kid my age in the poolroom. He was shooting pool and was really good. I made a mental note never to play him for money. We played each other shortly after the first time we'd met. When it was time to leave and pay for the time we played, we were told that Chink took care of it. And so began a lifelong relationship with Milty and Chink, who became my rabbi, the go-to guy when my gambling debts were beyond my means to pay.

Milty became my lifelong friend, best man at my wedding, and sometime business partner. I was with Milty at his bedside when he died some fifty years later.

Leaving Teller Avenue

Several years after my mother died and when my sisters were in college and my brother in high school, the family had outgrown our Teller Avenue apartment. We needed more rooms. My father found us an apartment on Morris Avenue, several blocks from Teller Avenue and two blocks closer to the Concourse. It was opposite Taft High School and on the same block as the Sugar Bowl, the local luncheonette where I could have great milkshakes and egg sandwiches and an on-premises bookie operation run by Moishe the Senator.

When I was a young boy, I loved reading stories by Damon Runyon. I loved the characters he wrote about. New York gamblers looking for an edge to make a score so they can make their next bet: Nathan Detroit, Sky Masterson, Nicely-Nicely Johnson, along with most of Runyon's likeable guys I could relate to, and with that in mind here are a few of my escapades from my early days growing up in the Bronx.

Hymie the Turk

In my poolroom days, the characters that congregated there were right out of a Damon Runyon novel. There was Sonny the Genius, Hymie the Turk, Moishe the Senator, Irv the Tooth. These were real guys. They all met down in this poolroom every day, where there was all sorts of action. Guys were shooting pool for money. They could bowl for money. There was a cardroom where gin or poker could be played every day. In the back of the poolroom, at the last pool table, Izzy Snow and his partner Smiling Artie were the bookmakers and would take bets on all sports action. It was a little Las Vegas where I spent many days shooting pool for money.

At home, we used to drink large glass bottles of sodas. I could get five cents deposit on a bottle. The empty bottles were left under the sink. When I gathered up twenty bottles, I'd take them down to Al Reisner's corner candy store, where I would get a dollar for returning the bottles and then head right down to College Rec Pool Room.

I used to take the dollar down to the poolroom and look to get into a pool game and see if I could run my dollar up. If I got into a game and won, I would win six dollars, take that six dollars, and find two basketball teams to bet on for a parley with Izzy Snow. If I got lucky and hit the two winners in the basketball games, I got myself eighteen dollars, and with eighteen dollars, I could get into the card game in the back room. I had all sorts of areas to maneuver in. It was exciting as hell. Every day was another adventure.

I remember one of my early capers got me real notoriety in the neighborhood. Across the street from the poolroom, there was the

Taft Sugar Bowl Luncheonette, where Hymie the Turk and Moishe the Senator took horse bets in the back booth. There was this big clock that was right over them. They would come at six o'clock every night and sit until eight o'clock, taking bets on the trotters. The first race would go off at eight o'clock, and they would stop taking bets at that time. I remember thinking to myself every time I made a bet with these guys, I knew they had an edge.

I wanted to beat these guys one time and came up with a plan. I got little Sam Raab, who lived on the corner of Morris Avenue and 170th Street right over a fruit store (I remember once throwing a watermelon right through the open window into his bedroom), and Lenny Tea in on the plan. Lenny Tea used to eat in the Taft Sugar Bowl every night at the same time. He would sit at the counter seven thirty, eating an egg salad sandwich and sipping a vanilla malted. He did this every night for the entire time I knew him. And then I got Ace Schwartz, truly one of the great lunatics of all times, who used to cross streets diagonally through busy intersections and never once looked at a light; he just kept going. Anyway, the plan that I put together with these guys was this:

Lenny Tea would sit at the counter, where he sat every night eating his sandwich, and for four straight nights, he would bet daily doubles at about five minutes to eight to set up a pattern with Hymie the Turk and Moishe the Senator. Hymie the Turk was one not to mess around with. He was known in the neighborhood for being Moishe's strong arm. He looked like and reminded me of Ernest Borgnine's character in *From Here to Eternity*. I never saw Hymie in a long-sleeved shirt. His forearms were like Popeye's, except hairier, and his shirt was never tucked in. He never smiled and was always taken very seriously.

Moishe the Senator probably got his name because of his stately manner. He was always well-groomed, had a full head of gray wavy hair, and dressed in expensive sports jacket and slacks. He always drove a new Cadillac. He was tall, and his most prominent feature was his large Jimmy Durante nose. Nobody dared mention the size of his nose in front of him.

The plan went into effect after four days of betting. On the fifth day, I went into the Sugar Bowl early in the morning when only the Spanish-speaking dishwasher was cleaning up and pushed the big clock back five minutes. He noticed, but after slipping him five dollars and putting my fingers to my lips and whispering shush, I knew he got the point.

That night, at seven thirty, Lenny Tea was at the counter, the same as always, eating his usual. Sam Raab and Ace Schwartz drove up to Yonkers Raceway earlier that evening. Ace Schwartz stayed in a gas station phone booth right across the highway from Yonkers Raceway. Sam Raab went into the parking lot of Yonkers Raceway, where you could see the horses pass the finish line through the wooden picket fence. Sam Raab, hanging on to the fence, watched the first race go off and saw the 3 horse win the race. He turned around and flashed his hand up in the air three times, signaling to Ace Schwartz that it was the 3 horse that won.

Ace Schwartz was on the phone with me. I was in the drugstore diagonally across the street from the Sugar Bowl in a phone booth talking with Schwartz while all of this was going on. I hung up the phone, ran across the street, and told Lenny Tea it was the 3 horse. Now mind you, the first race is over, and Hymie and Moishe don't know it's over because it's before eight o'clock, according to the big clock on the wall. Lenny Tea, knowing the winner, goes and makes a series of daily double bets, wheeling the double, and betting the horse to win in the first race for sizable money. I can't even remember exactly how much it was, but we won. We got away with it. We won about four hundred dollars, which we split. Back in the '50s, four hundred dollars was a ton of money.

But more than winning the money was the fact that we pulled it off. We did it, and everybody knew. Even Hymie the Turk knew it because he came to me a couple of days after we pulled it off and told me, "Hey, fellow, you better quit when you're a winner."

I got the message. Never again, at least not with Hymie.

Past Posting Again

After past posting (betting on the winner when the race is over) Hymie the Turk and Moishe the Senator, I attempted that scheme again, without success, when I found a bar that a guy told me about on 165th Street in the Bronx in a different neighborhood from mine. It was a bar where, only on Monday nights, a bookmaker would take bets on the trotters up in Yonkers. These races would be televised at nine o'clock. When I heard about this, I was really excited because it gave me the option to bet and watch the races on TV when I could not make the track.

It was a bar full of working guys. They were truck drivers, cab drivers, and big burly drinking guys. They were drinkers, not really gamblers, but they would kill a Monday night by betting with their behind-the-bar bookmaker. When I went there the first time, I couldn't believe what I was seeing. At nine o'clock, the television coverage started with the third race live. After the third race was over, they televised on tape the first and second races, which had already run.

The bookmaker was taking bets on the taped races. He would let people bet with him at nine thirty, when the race was already over at eight o'clock. These guys were sitting there, drinking anyway and betting races that were already run. They were in a world by themselves. I couldn't believe it. So I bet that Monday and couldn't wait until next week when I ran back and this guy was still taking these bets.

I can't let this go by, I thought. So I called up Normie Davis, a skinny kid who lived around the block from me and was going to

City College. He was the only one in the neighborhood I knew who had a car. I tell him about the bar and how this bookmaker is taking bets on the first and second race after they were run. I tell him that we are going to past post this bookmaker and beat him for a lot of money. I get Normie crazy, and he agrees to come with me on this scheme.

We bet every Monday for three weeks, setting up the book-maker. On the fourth Monday, we decided to put this plan into effect. We drove up to Yonkers Raceway, got the winner of the first race and drove back to the bar, arriving in time to bet the horse that won the first race, and we bet all the horses in the second race to win the daily double. This is known as wheeling. I remember that we were sitting watching the taped races. Stupidly, Normie and I were acting pretty casual for having just hit the double and winning about 250 dollars.

I heard a little grumbling from the other end of the bar, where the bookmaker was sitting, and started to feel very uncomfortable. I say to Normie, "I think we should stay, bet another twenty dollars, lose some money back, and then pick up our money and leave."

So we pick out a fifteen-to-one shot on the next race and bet twenty dollars to win on it, figuring the horse can't win. The race goes off, and this horse is running like he's Secretariat. Normie and I are screaming and jumping up and down. The horse wins and pays thirty-two dollars. We can't believe we picked a winner and that the bookmaker now owes us about 550 dollars.

I go over to collect, and the bookmaker says, "There's something wrong here. You guys were too calm watching the double. You're going to have to kick my ass if you want this money."

I wasn't about to kick his ass knowing that thirty guys were there who would have loved to beat the shit out of us. Before we backed out the door I asked him for the money that I bet. He said, "Get lost, kids."

He was right. I was sixteen.

As we were walking to the car, I'm getting crazy and said, "I can't believe this guy wouldn't give us our money. We conned him, and he took our bets." I couldn't believe he wouldn't do what Hymie did. Hymie let us keep the money, but this guy wasn't playing fair in my mind.

I was so crazy that I went to Billy the Bull's house. Billy was the local tough guy in my neighborhood. I said to Billy, "Listen, I'll cut you in for a third of this 550 dollars owed to me. We got to get this money."

I psych up Billy the Bull, and we jump into the car and go back to the bar. By the time I psych Billy up, it was two hours later, and Normie says, "Just let's forget it. Let's just forget it."

He was the only sensible one there. Luckily for us, everyone had cleared out of the bar when we arrived. They had all gone home. Who knows what would have happened had they still been there.

The next morning clearer heads prevailed, and I put it behind me. I guess you just can't pull these schemes off successfully all the time.

Florence and Queens

We were living on Morris Avenue when my father died. I was sixteen and finished high school. Florence finished college and was teaching. Lenny was several months away from getting married. What to do with the apartment and sixteen-year-old Bobby? It was decided that we would give up the apartment and that I would temporarily stay with Florence. Florence found an apartment in Flushing, Queens, which she was going to share with a schoolteacher-friend. It was tough. I didn't want to live in Queens and didn't want to live with my sister and her roommate. It was a disaster from the get-go.

Florence tried to make up for the losses in my life and give me direction. She wanted me to go to college like she and Genie did, not like my brother Lenny, who enlisted in the army as soon as he graduated from high school. Florence wanted me to be able to make a living, get an education, get married, be a mensch.

I could care less. I wanted to do what I wanted when I wanted to do it, the way it always was and still is. Being a mensch was not my calling as far as work. Otherwise, I'm a mensch.

But living with Florence was not my idea of a life. It got to the point where if I didn't call her and tell her I wasn't coming home and didn't come home for a night or two, she'd bring out our extended family—the Kronishes, assorted aunts, uncles, cousins, and their kin—to join forces with the local police precinct to track me down.

The last straw came when, after a weekend of gambling and girlfriends, I made my way back to Queens. No need for a key to let me in. When I got home, Florence, the Kronishes, and cops were there to greet me along with a contingent of neighbors and passersby. Florence was in a state of collapse. The Kronish clan and cops heaved a sigh of relief and eventually left. I remember an onlooker neighbor shaking her head and saying, "Florence will have to do something with that boy"—meaning, me. *Not to worry*, I heard the voice in my head saying. *Bobby, you gotta get out of here.*

You're in the Army Now

The only way out I saw for me would be the army. I wouldn't have to live with my sister, and I could put off paying Sugar Bowl's head bookie Moishe the Senator what I owed him until I got out.

It was 1959 when I enlisted in the army. It was six years after the end of the Korean War, and the US was experiencing peace and prosperity. Everyone was watching *Father Knows Best*, *Your Show of Shows* starring Sid Caesar. Phil Silvers was playing Sergeant Bilko, who was spoofing the army. All was good with no signs of any fighting or war, except for the Cold War with Russia. That appeared to be all political with no real danger imminent.

There was still the obligatory draft call-up for all healthy and eligible young men between the ages of eighteen and thirty. If drafted, you were required to do two years' active duty to fulfill your obligation. There was an option for those who did not want to spend two years of active duty. You could join the army reserves, which allowed you to do only six months active duty. However, you were committed to six years of being a reservist. Since it was peacetime, just about every upwardly mobile college grad joined a reserve outfit to beat the draft, and that included me, a non-college-educated seventeen-year-old gambler.

This plan, for many of the reservists, backfired when President Kennedy called back the reserves to prepare for the war with Russia. It wasn't called a war; it was a crisis—the Berlin Crisis. It ended in a year with no shots being fired. Needless to say, that year for many of the reservists was a miserable time, pulled away from family and blossoming careers. To them, it was just a wasted year with no understanding of why.

What we didn't realize at the time and for many years was that this action might have saved tens of thousands of reservists' lives. It seems when the Berlin Crisis ended, something was starting to happen in a part of the world that many of us in the United States never heard of: Vietnam. Because we did our duty serving our country during the Berlin Crisis, we were exempt from active duty fighting the Vietnam War. There is no question in my mind that, if it wasn't for the Berlin Crisis, I and many of the hundreds of thousands of reservists would have been called to fight in Vietnam, and if I had been drafted, I would have gone to fight. That's the way it was then. WWI, WWII, the Korean War—guys were called to serve the country, and they went. No protesting, no running to Canada, no finagling a way out—you did your duty. You served your country.

All I wanted was to be out of Queens, free from my sister's watchful eyes, and to delay having to pay off the bookie with money I didn't have. It was a debt that would be paid eventually, or I'd serve a lifetime of permanent disability.

Fort Dix, New Jersey, was where I was sent for basic training. Because I was living in Queens, the closest place to enlist for the reserves was in Long Island City in Queens. I wasn't scared, just squeamish and thinking that I'd made the right choice for a seventeen-year-old who had only gambling and girls on his mind. Basic training lasted two months before I was off to Fort Gordon in Georgia for MP (military police) training.

Looking back—and at the time—two months' basic training in Fort Dix was a piece of cake for me. I was young, in good shape, and doing daily sit-ups and push-ups. No big deal. Even the zingers and bullying from the sergeants was tolerable, maybe even comical. I wasn't intimidated, and Georgia's Fort Gordon was no big deal, I thought.

I arrived at MP training at my company on Friday, two days ahead of schedule, and was assigned to a barracks with other recruits. Official training would start on Monday, and we were on our own until then. There I was on the Friday before the big Monday in a barracks with a bunch of Southern guys. They were happy as hell to be on their way to living their dream as they gleefully echoed, almost in unison, "I'm in the army now. I'm in the army now."

Clearly, we were cut from a different cloth. I was the only recruit who intended to do his six months' duty and be on my way back to the outside world. And that wasn't the only difference between us. I was from the North and the only Jewish guy in the outfit, and they knew it. They would call out to me, "Hey, you a Jew voice, a Jew face?"

I couldn't understand a thing they said. They couldn't understand a thing I said. All they heard was my "Jew voice" and saw my "Jew face." So I spent all weekend spit polishing my boots and shining the brass buckle on my narrow belt. On Sunday, we all reported to the orderly room to fill out paperwork. I noticed a list posted on the wall with the names of the unit's recruits. All names were handwritten in black ink, except for "Ochs," which was in red ink. *Can't be good*, I thought. *Can't be good.*

At four that Monday morning, the unit was called out into a formation. It was pitch-black of night, and there we were standing outside. The sergeant was ready to inspect his troop. I was feeling on top of my game, knowing that I had the cleanest, shiniest boots and brass buckle of anyone after spending two straight days of doing nothing but spit polishing them.

As the sergeant made his way down the line of trainee recruits, he screamed and hissed that boots were dirty, and he wanted to know why they weren't shined. When he got to me, he put his booted foot between my two boots in the pitch-dark. You couldn't see a thing, let alone a black boot. He yelled in my face, "Hey, soldier, why didn't you polish your boots? How come?"

Smart alecky, I retorted, "Didn't have the time, Sir. Didn't have the time."

Stunned, he grabbed me and threw me out of the formation, screaming, "You New York Jew boy, you will learn how to be a soldier."

For a week after that, I got handed every shitty detail they could come up with, and the sergeant let me know, "It ain't gonna stop."

I got the message. I had to do something and went to the company commander and explained to him, with all the sincerity I could muster, that I truly wanted to be an MP and use the training to become a police officer when I got out of the army. I went on that I had an explosive temper and wanted it on my record that, when I became an MP on duty and carrying a loaded .45, if anyone called me a "dirty Jew bastard," I'd blow their fucking head off.

Half knowing I was full of it, he asked, "Can you type?"

"Absolutely," I responded. Fact is, I never laid a hand on a typewriter, let alone touched a typewriter key.

"Good," he said. "You're transferred to Headquarters Company. Now get the hell out of here."

What a coup! Headquarters Company. Boy, did I luck out. There was nothing like being in Army Headquarters. In Headquarters, you were treated like royalty. When I arrived there, the colonel asked me what I did before enlisting. "Mostly gambling," I said.

"Okay, you're in charge of running the company's football, basketball, baseball pools."

I was on a roll.

Army's Over, and I'm Out

Old neighborhood, same old same old

After six months, active duty was over. I was back in New York and had to find my own apartment. No more living with my sister in Queens or any place with anyone else. I found myself a one-bedroom apartment on Clarke Place in my old Bronx neighborhood, a block west of the Grand Concourse, not too far from my old gambling haunts and several blocks from 167th Street, where my father had had his dental business. Familiar turf. Good to be back.

Once I was back living in the Bronx, I was in action every day, betting on something I could find: baseball, basketball, football, horses, cards, dice—anything. And that came with some crazy superstitions: if I was losing and if I was betting with one bookmaker, I would try and find another bookmaker to change my luck. It was crazy but true.

Anyway, I had found this bookmaker Marty Fink, who rented an apartment on Southern Boulevard in East Bronx, where he took bets. I started betting with him, and I remember I won a Friday night baseball game. Saturday morning, I planned to go over to Marty Fink to collect my money and make another bet. As I was leaving, there was a knock on the door, and it's Albie Morgus.

Albie Morgus was a strange guy, and we had a strange type of relationship. I didn't care for him, and I am sure that he didn't care for me. He would hang around and watch me gamble. When he found out whom I was betting on, he would root against me. For some weird reason, I kind of enjoyed that. I enjoyed the fact that if I did win, it would aggravate this guy. I loved to aggravate him. He loved to aggravate me. That was our relationship.

So there is Albie Morgus appearing at my door and wanting to know what I am going to do for the day. I tell him I won a bet the night before, and I am planning to go over to Marty Fink to make a bet with the money I won. He says, "Can I come?"

I said, "Sure."

Albie Morgus, who never made a bet in his life, wants to come with me to the bookmaker. So we drive over to Southern Boulevard, and I am trying to think of which team I am going to bet for the day. This pitcher is going, that one is going. Marachel is going, Koufax is going, Whitey Ford is also pitching—everybody is going, and I'm figuring out who I'm going to bet.

Marty Fink's building was in an all-Spanish-speaking neighborhood. And now Albie and I are walking up the stairs to the fifth-floor apartment. I am studying the newspaper. At every landing, there is a group of Spanish-speaking people there, looking up and babbling away. It was a little odd to me, but it didn't dawn on me that something was fishy.

Finally, I got upstairs and knocked on the door. Marty usually had on his side of the door a goon looking out to make sure only the right people came in. So now the door swings open, and instead of one goon, there are two goons standing there dressed in suits and ties. They grab me and Albie. They pull us into the apartment, and the guy says, "We're the police." (No shit. Who else wears suits and ties?) "What are you guys doing here?"

I tell him that I understand that this apartment is for rent, and I am looking for an apartment. He gives me a push against the wall and says, "We don't want no wise guys here," and he shoves me into the other room. Albie comes flying in after me, and there is a whole group of guys waiting there. It seems that the police came and raided Marty Fink and were collecting as many of his customers as they could.

After they collected about twenty guys, they handcuffed us and took us down the stairs, where there were two paddy wagons waiting.

We filed into them, and they took us off to the Tremont Avenue Jail, where they put us in a large holding pen that fit all of us. We were supposed to hole up in there until seven o'clock that night and then be taken down to night court.

So now we are in this big pen, twenty degenerate gamblers, and it's like twelve or one o'clock in the afternoon. We are all a little punchy and not sure what's what. I think this thing is not serious and that by the time we hit night court, they will throw it out. No big deal.

Now a cop comes around, and I start talking to him at the gate, and he says, "I'm going out to get something. Anybody want some sandwiches or coffee? If you guys have some money, I'll get some sandwiches."

The cop is already being our pal, so I said, "Sure."

We all ordered sandwiches and coffee and I said, "Go get some dice and cards."

The cop didn't even flinch. He went out and got us sandwiches, coffee, dice, and cards. We started a hot crap game right in the jail, and some guys started to play cards. I said, "This is terrific." I didn't even feel like I was in jail. We were doing what we wanted to do anyway.

But Albie, he couldn't enjoy himself. The guy was crazy. All he kept on worrying about was that he's in jail and that his mother would find out. This guy still lives with his mother. So now, seven o'clock rolls around, and the game is interrupted, and they are taking us down to night court. They handcuff us up again, and we go back into paddy wagons, and they drive us down to the Tombs. The Tombs is where they hold people who were just arrested before you get to see the judge.

The Tombs in New York, on a Saturday night, is a place to behold. It's like a zoo. We are thrown into this pen, and guys were coming in with their ears ripped off, telling us that their wives had smacked them in the head with the phone. Their noses were broken, and they were bleeding. It was a mixture of these crazy people and us.

Now I was getting a little annoyed. Seven o'clock led to eight o'clock, and eight o'clock let to nine o'clock, and it doesn't look like we are going to see the judge until eleven o'clock or midnight. I'm pissed off. I missed the trotters, and it's getting a little inconvenient.

But better than that is Albie Morgus is really getting crazy. The man is berserk. He doesn't know what to do. He says, "My mother cooked dinner. She won't know where I am. She's going to call the police."

I say, "Good. She'll find you."

He says, "She's not supposed to know. I want to call my mother. I don't know what to do. I can't call my mother. They won't let me call."

That was the only thing that kept me rolling along there. Without Albie, I might have gone a little crazy myself, but with Albie being so aggravated, it was a pleasure.

Anyway, the cops downstairs at the Tombs tell us we should all plead guilty, that it's going to be some sort of misdemeanor thing, and we should all plead guilty to unlawful assembly. It will be a twenty-five-dollar fine, and we will all go home. We go upstairs to the judge, who was babbling away. I wasn't even listening or paying attention until he said, "Twenty-five-hundred-dollar bail, each man."

That I heard, and if you don't have it, you have to stay two nights until Monday, when the trial will be held. We didn't have 2,500 dollars for the whole twenty of us put together. Now they march us downstairs again, fingerprint us, and process us into individual cells. I started to play all the Humphrey Bogart and James Cagney movies in my mind. All those jail movies, and now I'm in jail for real. We spend the night in jail.

The next day, a friend came to the rescue and bailed me out. On Monday, we went to court for this cockamamie case. The judge calls the first guy who gets up and goes through his song and dance. After hearing about five guys, the judge dismissed the case and sent everyone home—no fines. End of that story for me.

Conrad

The year was 1960, a little over sixty years ago. I was eighteen and just out of the army. I had no clue as to what was ahead in my future. My brother owned a bar and restaurant in the Stadium Motor Lodge, a motel off the Major Deegan Expressway and 167th Street, a half mile from Yankee Stadium. Needing to make a buck, my brother suggested to me that I work as a bartender at his restaurant temporarily to make some money to help pay my bills and until I found out what I wanted to do with my life.

Before actually working at the bar, I had to learn what to do, so I was trained to be a bartender by Conrad the head bartender. He was a Black man from Barbados and was a professionally trained bartender from a five-star hotel in Barbados before moving to the States to find his American dream.

Conrad made sure that I got a first-class course on being a first-class bartender—no nonsense. I learned the basics first: squeezing lemons for lemon juice, making simple syrup sweetener of equal parts sugar and boiled water. These were the base ingredients for most mixed drinks that were shaken and not stirred. Then there were the stirred drinks: martini, Manhattan, Rob Roy.

I don't care what James Bond said. I wonder how many bartenders today actually know how to make a classic martini. Back in my day, when someone ordered a martini, you filled a mixing glass with ice, added one part dry vermouth and two parts gin (yes, gin, not vodka, unless asked for). Then stir at least thirty times around, thus properly chilling the drink. Then pour into a chilled three-and-

46

a-half-ounce glass (V-shaped stem) with olive (onion—Gibson—or lemon twist only if requested). We charged seventy-five cents for a martini at the Stadium Lounge.

Today, if you order a martini, the mixologist (no longer bartender) immediately pulls out a nearby shaker glass. This martini is now about sixteen dollars per, depending on the restaurant.

Over the years, the vermouth disappeared. Vodka replaced gin, and the drink is shaken, not stirred, which bruises the cocktail because of the ice particles.

Once I learned to make all the drinks with their correct garnish and the proper glass to put them in, I was ready to go behind the bar. I was a little nervous at first and asked Conrad, "What if someone asks me for a drink that I didn't know?" His reply was that after what he taught me, if I hadn't heard of the drink, for sure, whoever ordered this drink knows even less. So just smile and mix anything together, top it with an orange and a cherry, and they are sure to love it. I'm not sure that would work with today's savvy clientele, but that was my start in the restaurant business sixty years ago in the Bronx at the Stadium Motor Lodge.

At the Stadium Motor Lodge, breakfast, lunch, and dinner were served, but the real money was made at night, serving drinks until four in the morning. We had trios playing live music nightly, and because we were close to Yankee Stadium, Yankee players like Phil Linz, Tony Kubek, Tex Clevenger had rooms at the motel and would hang out at the bar, which attracted young women, which attracted me in turn.

Food at the restaurant became an adjunct, a promotional tool. Although the food was good, it was not the reason people were coming. One of our best promotional campaigns was when we offered a one-night-only seven-and-eleven-cent dinner on the opening night of the Al Nero trio. We served a fried chicken dinner with fries for seven cents and a sliced steak dinner with fries for eleven cents. Needless to say, the place was packed that night and many nights thereafter at regular menu prices.

It was clear to me that the restaurant business was not just about food but about creating a scene where people would get together and socialize. Yes, the food and service had better be first-rate in order to sustain. But it's the crowd that creates the energy, the heartbeat, to give it life and to keep it going.

There's no question that things have changed over the years, but I'm not certain for the better when it comes to bars and restaurants. I suppose that some restaurant owner today might write a similar article sixty years from now, expressing their views on the restaurant business.

The Stadium Motor Lodge catered to New York's baseball teams, the Yankees and the Mets, and was a popular stopover for car dealers from the south. The car dealers who hung out at the bar were old-time bigots. They constantly made racial remarks to Conrad, who just grinned, not smiled, and never said a word. He'd just laugh. One day, I couldn't take it anymore, and said, "Conrad, why do you put up with those racist assholes?"

"Bobby," he said, "when they wake up in the morning with a hangover after a night at the bar with me bartending and they look for the money they spent on drinking the night before, that's the money I earned and went in my pocket. That's how I put up with it." This time he smiled. More Bartending 101, and a lesson I learned well, not only in bartending but in running restaurants and life.

It was 1961, and it was one year since I'd been out of army active duty. As I was settling into my new job and a new apartment, world events were swirling. The Berlin Crisis was in the air. President Kennedy and Russia's Nikita Khrushchev had tanks facing off against each other. As the paint was drying on the walls of my Clarke Place apartment, I got notice that I was being called up to active duty. That was part of the deal I'd signed on for when I enrolled in the reserves two years earlier, and it meant I could be on active duty for the next four years.

Future on Hold, Back to Barracks

And so I was returning to my old 310 MP Battalion, which had orders to fly to Fort Bragg, North Carolina, the home of the Eighty-Second Airborne. Fort Bragg had the reputation for having the worst crimes of all army posts. It was the first time since the Korean War that reserve units were being reactivated, and that could mean only one thing: the US was going to war. No more civilian life, no get-out date for me.

There was complete chaos when our unit arrived in Fort Bragg. Our unit was in a barracks that hadn't been used since World War II and were not in good shape. Our Battalion was made up of companies A, B, C, and Headquarters. Each unit had its own barracks. A, B, C was known as line company and were for infantry foot soldiers who trained for battle every day and did all the grunt work. Our battalion took over policing of the fort.

The MP company that was originally there was sent to Berlin. My assignment was to company A. From my own experience, I knew that Headquarters was the cushiest deal, so I took my duffel bag and moved into Headquarters barracks. Everyone there had a specific job—cook, engineer, motor pool—except me. No one bothered the guys in Headquarters. I didn't have a job or qualifications for any job. Most importantly, I wasn't assigned to be there. Since nobody knew if we would be going to war or when we'd be getting the hell out of there, I didn't much care. My first morning in Headquarters, I woke up as all of the other companies were marching off to war games and policing the post, which had the worst crime record.

As company A was in formation, the sergeant called out, "Ochs." No answer.

He moved on to the next name, while I was in bed, figuring out what to do. Unlike my unit in Fort Gordon, this reserve unit was made up of guys from New York. Most of us knew each other in one way or another, known as six degrees of separation, where everybody knows somebody or somebody who knows somebody, which made it easier for me to be myself and to make my moves.

I had no problem getting breakfast in the mess hall or eating and bullshitting to kill time with the cooks, but I couldn't do that all day, so I found myself a wrench, put a dirty rag in my back pocket, and strolled up and down the company streets. Chutzpah, I had plenty of. Whenever an officer or sergeant passed me and asked, "Ochs, what are you doing?" I'd point to my wrench and say that I was "stringing wire with engineering."

That worked for a few days until one sergeant grabbed me and took me to the officer in charge of engineering and asked if I was assigned to him. "No," he said, "but I can use him." The first thing he told me to do was to climb a giant pole to the top. Not one for climbing poles, I asked to go back to company A, and he sent me back to company A barracks where I was revered by the New York recruits as the company's comedian.

Morale there sucked. I mean it was really, really low. These twenty-something-year-old guys were pulled out of their jobs, away from their wives and young families, and called to active duty. Their careers were on hold for nobody knew how long. They were scared, angry, miserable. I was at least six years younger than these guys, unmarried, and I didn't have any obligations. I brought energy to the surroundings.

To their credit, the top brass took notice, and I was given some leeway to lighten things up to bring levity to the guys in the barracks. To this day, Jerry Rosenzweig, one of the recruits, remembers and always thanks me for having made those terrible times bearable. I was a cutup. Jerry's remained a friend.

Barrack Boys Go Broadway

O ne day in October of the year we were called up, a higher-up came into the barracks and said that the service club would be putting on a talent show and wanted to know if any of us guys in the barracks wanted to audition. Without missing a beat, I began doing my shtick, jumping around and riffing on top of my lungs, "Let's write a Christmas show à la Mickey Rooney and Judy Garland," bellowing on top of my lungs. The guys were laughing and repeating what I was saying.

The next thing I knew two of the guys in the barracks, Paul Amorelli, who was a graphic artist from Queens, and Chuck Weiss, who was a theatrical agent at William Morris from Manhattan, were scribbling down dialogue and songs for what turned out to be a Christmas show. I would be the sad sack soldier who wanted to go home on Christmas pass and would be reciting a poem to the tune of "The Night Before Christmas." We wrote four songs and used the music and lyrics of popular songs to spoof life in the call up reserves. In less than a week, we finished.

Since it was the beginning of October, it would be the perfect Christmas show for our outfit. We pitched the idea to Battalion Commander Colonel Westervelt. He liked it and set up a backers audition with the top officers on the post two days after we met with him. He told us we'd have to perform the show to a roomful of generals, colonels, their aides, and the chaplain of the post, which was great, except we had no idea what we were doing, and there was no time to structure anything. It would have to be a reading. We would need musicians. So John Signorelli from our company, who played guitar, brought on Mario Caruso, who played piano and was another recruit from the barracks. We had no rehearsals. We just did the reading and sang the songs. The bigwig backers and the chaplain loved it and approved our doing the show the next night at the officers' club, which was the Copacabana of the post. Opening night was a hoot. Everyone and his wife showed up.

The club sat at least three hundred. There was a big stage. Behind the rows of seats in the audience was a kitchen. Chuck, Paul, and I came up with a plan. The musicians would start playing and singing. Luckily, we found out the night before that one of the recruits was a base player. I would stay in the kitchen in the back until it was my time to go on. It was a nail-biter for me. "Home for the Holidays" was my cue to go. Standing in the kitchen, I was hamstrung. We didn't plan for props, and I didn't know what to do. There was a mop, a pail, and a steel helmet within arm's reach. I grabbed the pail, filled it with the mop, and plopped the oversize helmet on my head. When it was my cue, I began moving slowly from the rear of the audience, stopping along the way as I approached the stage, mop, pail, and helmet all in place. My Emmett Kelly face stared forlornly at the audience. The house was roaring. A show and a star were born.

The next day's news of the show's success spread all over our base. The Fort Bragg newspaper gave us a rave review. We were an overnight sensation, the darlings of the base. We were given permission to devote all of our time to develop the show for Christmas, which was only two months away. While the show was intended for our battalion, every outfit on the post now wanted to see it. We were now "show people," and it was our job to create a full-blown show, and we did. We brought on more musicians, more songs, more shtick, better staging. Performing the show for troops from Maine to Florida was our tour of duty.

Silas Seandel, one of the other recruits, was originally in the chorus. He went on to play a sergeant in a sleeping gown and cap as he woke up the troops while singing, "It's going to be a great day," and doing tricks with a yo-yo, at which he's a pro.

Silas and I became good friends. When we weren't performing one week, we went off to the Masters Golf Tournament and stayed in a hotel on Main Street in Augusta, Georgia, where every conceivable character from all over the US-rented rooms to stay and see the Masters. In the hotel lobby, you could place a bet on your favorite golf player. There were women galore. Silas and I went to the Augusta National Golf Club every day. Recently, Silas and I were reminiscing. I recalled paying five dollars on Thursday and Friday and ten dollars on Saturday and Sunday in order to get in. Silas says we got in for free because we were in the army. No matter the price, we both remember it to be a great experience.

After the Christmas Show, we continued to entertain the troops. The *New York Times* magazine, in a four-page spread, reported how the show lifted the morale of the army reservists. Fortunately, there was never a war. Khrushchev blinked, and our last show was in August 1962, when we were sent home. Quite a mission for a bunch of New York recruits who came to serve their country. Now I asked myself, *What's next?*

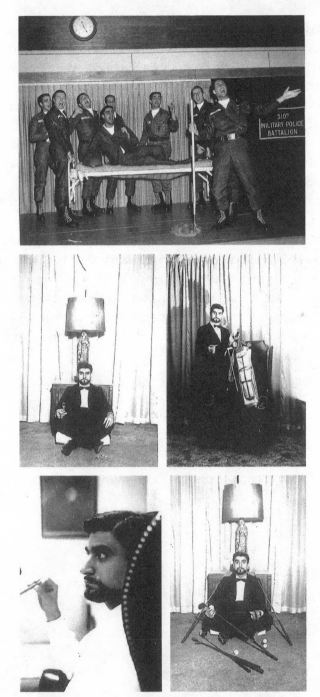

Bobby Ochs, United States Army show, 1962

Linda Eisenberg, Bobby Ochs, Clarke Place, Bronx, NY, 1962

Phil Serlin, Bobby Ochs, Clarke Place, Bronx, NY, 1962

Bronx Buddies in front of my Bronx apartment building, circa 1991
Bobby Ochs, Barry Sachs, Milty Cohen, Kenny Schwalb

Laughter in Reserve

While some of the Army Reservists called back into uniform grumble, and a House Armed Services subcommittee conducts hearings on the program, one outfit is laughing—by the numbers, of course—at its plight. A Reserve unit from Long Island City, the 310th Military Police Battalion, on active duty at Fort Bragg, N. C., has put together a musical spoof called "The Second Time Around." The M. P.'s playing the khaki circuit have been a hit all over the East and this week will entertain the U. S. O. national convention in Miami Beach.

SINGING COPS—The military chorus boys in "The Second Time Around"—a title describing the call-up of the Reserves—kid themselves in ten songs and skits. Pfc. Charles Weiss, producer and co-author of the show, is a Broadway theatrical agent; Pfc. John Signorelli, the musical director, is a guitarist.

(To tune of "See the U.S.A.")
Reservists one and all,
  We heard the new re-call,
The Army wants you back
  again, they say.
  The reason is the mess,
The world is in distress,
  As quoted by our buddy
    J. F. K.
And when we get out * * *
  It may be that we'll all re-up!

MONOLOGUE — At one point in the show, Pvt. Robert Ochs, shown here slightly out of uniform, recites the story of a soldier seeking a pass. He describes the perils in a parody of "'Twas the Night before Christmas."

'Twas the week before
  Christmas, and all
  through the Fort
A pass for the holidays
  was my only thought.
So I went to the Sergeant
  and said, "Sergeant Man,
I'd like to go home on a
  pass if I can."
And the Sergeant-man
  said, "At what do
  you drive?
Drop down on the floor—
  give me twenty-five!"

(Continued on Page 68)

Laughter In Reserve, New York Times Magazine

Here We Go Again Is Mood Of 310th Comedy Program

By SP4 STUART ELENKO

"The Second Time Around," the 310th MP Battalion's musical satire based on the recent recall of reservists to active duty, was given a sneak preview Saturday evening at the Ft. Bragg Officers Club.

The show was performed by a skeleton cast in the Lafayette Room for a large audience of officers and guests. This performance, directed produced and enacted by members of the 310th, proved a great surprise and success.

In the Broadway vernacular, the show was much like a backer's audition in that it was presented to gain public confidence and audience reaction. Captain Anthony Alt. Adjutant of the 310th MP Bn. remarked as he left the show: "In every sense of the word, it was fine entertainment. The lyrics and dialogue proved clever and witty, and at the same time, were presented in excellent taste."

The audience included 117

Military Police Officers and wives who were attending the M. P. Officers Christmas formal dance. Present were members of the Provost Marshal's offie and staff and company officers of the 310th 503rd, and 92d MP Battalions

along with MP representatives from 301st Log Command and the 82d Airborne Division.

Also present for the show were officers of various other units and their wives. Generally the audience lauded

(See Comedy Page 2A)

FAR FROM HOME -- Private Robert Ochs, (at microphone) asks for Christmas leave in high point of "The Second Time Around," a musical satire by members of the 310th MP Bn., based on the callup of reservists. The show was presented last Saturday for a special audience at the officers' club and will have its full-scale premiere next Thursday at Service Club #3.

Besides Ochs the cast includes (left to right) Pvt. Martin Litman, Sp-4 Jim Morrell, Pvt. John Signorelli and Pvt. Ralph Caruso. Others, not pictured, are PFC Paul Amorelli, Pvt. Mario Belfiore, Sp-4 Jerome Silverman and the show's writer, producer, director, PFC Charles Weiss. (U. S. Army Photo by Scroggins and Ostmark).

Here We Go Again is the mood of 310th comedy program

Army Duty Really Over, Back to a Gambling Life

After being discharged from the army, I returned home once again to my one-bedroom Bronx Clarke Place apartment, which still needed a painting. There are times in life when you have options as to what direction you want to or should go.

After my army show experience, where I was the star of a show, Chuck Weiss the William Morris` agent wanted to sign me on as a talent. I didn't take the offer. Doing the army show was fun and exciting. I loved it. It was a way to do what I wanted to do. Otherwise, I was just another soldier taking orders and doing what someone told me to do. That wasn't me, and I didn't have the desire and drive to be an actor.

I was nineteen and single and wanted to do whatever I wanted to do. Gambling gave me that lifestyle—action, freedom. So I gambled, gambled, gambled, spending my days betting every sport there was, including basketball, football, baseball, with the bookmaker and going off to the racetrack every night. When I made a big score, I bought me a brand-new 1962 White T-Bird with red bucket seats—a major chic magnate in those days. I was a man about town at twenty, still single, had my own apartment and a T-Bird. How could I miss? Girls galore came and went through my T-Bird and my apartment. I remember some; others, not. But like any gambler, I soon ran out of money, and reality kicked in. I needed a job.

Arnie Rosen, who bought the Stadium Motor Lounge from my brother Lenny, hired me as a bartender. After working a while as a bartender, Arnie asked me to manage the nightclub. The hours were from eight at night to four in the morning, which was perfect for me. I could go to the track during the day and work at the lounge at night. The Stadium Motor Lounge was a popular spot for singles, especially young and restless women. Imagine a twenty-year-old guy like me working in a nightclub with live music playing in the lobby of a motel with cocktail waitresses and women on the move. Most of my breaks were quickies in one of the motel rooms.

The Nightlife and First Love

Arnie Rosen was ten years older than me, married with two kids. He liked women and having his flings. Before buying the Stadium, he was a car dealer. His father left him some money, which gave Arnie a way to indulge his extramarital lifestyle. Arnie and I became fast friends. He always treated me as a partner and friend.

On a typical day, I'd get up around noon, and depending on my prior night's activity, I'd have breakfast at the Greek diner a few blocks from my apartment. I'd check out the newspaper to see if there were any horses at Aqueduct to bet and any games that I could bet on. Then I was off to the track.

At 6:00 p.m., I'd start my night of work at the lounge. My responsibilities and duties ranged from ordering food and liquor to hiring and scheduling staff and bands, as well as taking care of the books and cash and handling public relations and promotions. Simply said, I oversaw the operation. Of course, I was always the charmer in one of my many mohair suits and acted as host. At four in the morning when we closed for the night, Arnie and I and some of the cocktail waitresses went off to after-hours clubs, Chinatown for Chinese food, or Patsy's in Harlem for Italian at five in the morning or to one of the waitresses' homes to end the night.

Most of the guys I knew who were my age married their high school sweethearts, had kids, and nine-to-five jobs on either Wall Street or in the Garment Center. That was considered normal. If I had doubts about my lifestyle, I would go to the D train subway station at 170th Street and the Concourse in the morning after a night of clubbing and knocking around and would stand and watch the throng of people going down into the subway to their jobs. Nobody was smiling. They all looked miserable. Seeing them as a herd of sheep, I'd go back home and sleep till noon.

One night, while I was at the Stadium Lounge, a beautiful young girl walked in. She was looking for a waitress job. I took one look at her red hair, fair skin, legs that didn't stop, great body. I was dead—Rhonda Fleming come to life. Didn't matter if she never served a drink in her life. "You can start tomorrow," I said. That was it: Linda Bushn, my first love. The first shiksa in my life and the start of a hot and steamy love affair. Love, sex—all the same to this twenty-year-old and getting older. While I don't remember much that we talked about, I do remember the sex to this day, and that's more than fifty years later.

Our affair started instantly. Working together intensified everything. We spent day and night together and couldn't keep our hands off each other—not good when you have to work. I was consumed. I wasn't thinking straight, if I was thinking at all. Linda was nineteen, coming off a divorce. She had two infants to support. Didn't matter. I decided we should get married. Linda was more levelheaded and said she needed someone more stable and financially reliable than I was, not a gambler working in a nightclub. I still tried to convince her, but she resisted.

One morning, in frustration, I said, "Let's take a ride. I need to calm down." We got into my car. I thought the only way I could marry her would be to elope. I headed over the George Washington Bridge to the New Jersey Turnpike south. I didn't know where I was going but figured when we got to Maryland, we would find someone to marry us. In those days, the age for getting married was younger in Maryland than in New York, and Maryland was popular for eloping teens where you didn't need a blood test.

While driving on the turnpike, Linda realized I was serious. She got nervous and panicked. She didn't want to be kidnapped and swept away by this knight in a shining T-Bird. But I kept driving. She kept screaming, "Turn around. Turn around."

Somewhere around Delaware, I came to my senses and turned back to New York. Linda was overwhelmed by the act of this desperate, crazed man and decided we were meant for each other and said, "Let's get married."

We picked a wedding date. I'd arrange for us to get married in Caesars Palace in Las Vegas, and Izzy Snow, the bookie, would make all the arrangements. His brother Leibel had a big job running Caesars Palace, and everything would be VIP.

I found us a two-bedroom apartment in Yonkers, a five-minute drive to Yonkers Raceway, where we would live after we got married. The night before we were to fly off to Vegas, Arnie Rosen threw us a big party at the Stadium Lounge. The whole staff and many of the regular customers were there to congratulate and wish us luck. It was a great party.

When it was over, Linda and I went back to my Clarke Place apartment, and after passionate, hot, steamy sex, we were quiet—too quiet. I turned to her and said this isn't going to work. She looked at me and nodded. The thought of being tied down to marriage with two ready-made kids got to me. I was petrified of what I was getting into. And poof! Just like that, it was over. As someone set to music, "It was just one of those things, just one of those magical flings, a trip to the moon on gossamer wings, just one of those crazy things."

And so it ended. It took a while for the flame to burn out, and after calling off the honeymoon and Yonkers apartment, I went back to working at the Stadium Motor Lodge. Linda met an older, more established guy, who owned a fleet of taxis. They moved to Long Island and hopefully lived happily ever after.

For a while, there were several other women in and out of my life. Can't remember any or many of them, at least not until I booked the Al Nero trio to play the Stadium Lounge. The trio consisted of Al Nero on piano, Sonny Kerr on drums (who dealt grass on the side), and Susan Scott on stand-up base. They all sang. They were a good group. When they would do a set, I sat at a table and watched and listened. It wasn't so much the group that interested me. It was Susan Scott. I couldn't keep my eyes off her. She was the complete opposite of Linda in many ways. She was almost petite and, standing next to her stand-up base, appeared even smaller than she was. She had short auburn hair, dark eyes, a pretty face, and a great body. What attracted me most was her voice. When she sang and played that base, she never smiled, like Keely Smith. She was all in.

It wasn't long before the two of us hooked up. In the nightclub business, at the end of the night, like at four in the morning, it's the cocktail waitresses you're drawn to or maybe some hottie with the hots who would wait it out for me at the bar. So it was natural for Susan and I to get it on. A drink, breakfast, an after-hours drinking pub—the next thing you know, you're in bed together. Gambling, women, all-nighters were what my life was about.

Susan came from a wealthy cattle-owning family in Colorado. She was graduated from Wellesley College with honors and was really intelligent. After college, she came to New York and joined the Al Nero trio. She was very liberal politically, a freethinker. She introduced me to smoking weed. This was in the early '60s, when young women were usually pushed down the road to get married, to have children, and to be the perfect housewife—not Susan.

So there we were, Susan standing with her base as the band played and I in my mohair suit. When it was over for the night, we would end up at her apartment getting stoned, listening to the Beatles ("Norwegian Wood"), and screwing all night. In the morning, we drove to the country or the beach. Gambling and betting on a horse never crossed my mind, except when I took off for Belmont. And so it went until one day, when Susan said, "I'm leaving," and did.

Back again to my old routine, which now included smoking weed occasionally. Sometimes, because of my new found indulgence, things got a little cloudy. I'm not sure of the sequence of events, but soon after Susan left, I decided to take time out from work. I just felt like I needed time away and, like all gamblers who aren't working and have no cash flow, there comes a time when you go broke. I didn't want to go back to the Stadium Lounge. On to the next *what's next?*

Bobby Ochs, Linda Bushn, Arnie's date, and Arnie
Rosen, Empire Room Waldorf Astoria, 1963

Time Out at Green Mansions

In those days, when everyone my age was going to Fire Island or the Hamptons or the Catskills on the weekends, I was at home sleeping through most of the day and running around with cocktail waitresses all night or going to the track. It would be a good change to get out of the city. And with some gambling IOUs outstanding, I thought it best to check out for the summer. A friend suggested I get a job at Green Mansions as a bartender, and I did.

Green Mansions was a resort in upstate New York, a little north of Lake George and Saratoga Race Track—the perfect setting for me. It was on a private lake surrounded by bungalows, and from Memorial Day to Labor Day, the hotel's bungalows were filled with young singles on vacation who were looking to score or meet their forever match. There were like five hundred women and maybe two hundred men who came to spend their one-week vacations. The men were unmarried, professional, eligible. The women came to find their *bashert*, preferably a doctor or a lawyer.

Although I didn't fit the male profile, I couldn't lose with those odds. When I got there, I immediately hooked up with a waitress on staff. Because I was a bartender who would be pouring drinks for him, the chef, who was German, invited me to join him and his kitchen staff to have all my meals at the chef's table.

Eating at the chef's table was a big deal. You ate better than the paying guests. You name it, you got it. Steaks, chops, lobsters—the perks of sitting at the chef's table. We ate in the guest dining room. Tables had linen napkins and silver—only the best. The guest dining room was on one side of the kitchen. The staff dining room—where the servers, busboys, dishwashers ate—was on the opposite side. Of course, they did not eat the same quality or type of food or get the same preparation as the chef's table. No table linen, no napkins, no silver—only a stark wooden room with wood tables and chairs. Who cared?

After one week of five-star luxury dining with the chef and his cooks, I found myself walking through the staff dining room, through the kitchen, and into the guest dining room, where I saw this really cute staffer smiling at me. She was sitting at a table with another waitress. I could smell the kashe varnishkes with mushrooms they were eating. I smiled back and couldn't help but stare at her 36D breasts bursting out of a tight-fitting starched white shirt. I grabbed a plate of kashe varnishkes for myself and sat down with Nancy Hunt, a college girl working a summer job. Who could resist that face, the beautiful well-rounded boobs, and a plate of kashe varnishkes? That was the end of my steak dinners. I never returned to the chef's table.

Summer of Loves

The next few weeks and through the summer, Nancy and I had incredible sex whenever and wherever we could: in the lake, on shore after midnight swims, in the dining room linen closet, sometimes even in bed. And I didn't have much time to explore other options, nor was I looking, not until I found myself attracted to Lois Zetter.

Green Mansions was known for their theater group. The staff produced and put on shows every week for the resort's guests. It was summer stock, and the young staff was made up of talented and aspiring actors and actresses. They came to perform and hone their craft. Lois Zetter was a member of the ensemble. So was Madeline Kahn, with whom I had a memorable encounter. My room that summer was in a huge old two-story Victorian house on the grounds of Green Mansions. It had maybe six bedrooms. Mine was on the second floor across the hall from Madeline's. The main floor had a large living room and kitchen.

There was a large potbelly stove in the living room near the front door, which heated the entire house. It was summer, and heat wasn't generally needed, but it was cold one particular night, and I was returning home. As I entered the living room to get to the stairs, I was startled by something moving on the floor next to the potbelly stove. It was dark. Could be an animal, I thought, and I instinctively turned on the light.

It wasn't an animal. It was Madeline Kahn wrapped in a blanket, trying to get warm. She told me her room was too cold, so she decided to sleep on the floor next to the stove. We talked, and I asked if she wanted to stay in my room and share my bed, which was right over the potbelly stove. She said yes but that nothing sexual would go on, just sleeping. Hmm, I'd heard that before. So we climbed into bed.

Within minutes, I was aroused and started making my moves. She started yelling and hitting me and jumped out of bed and left. I never found out if she went back to her cold room or to the potbelly stove downstairs. We had no interaction for the rest of the summer. Bad move on my part, but I didn't see it that way at the time.

Years later, Madeline Kahn had some great movie roles in *Blazing Saddles*, *Young Frankenstein*, and *What's Up, Doc?* And when I owned my first restaurant, Samantha, she came by and we spoke a while. Madeline Kahn had an illustrious career in film, TV, and theater and died too young in 1999.

Lois Zetter was a college graduate a couple years older than me. She was attractive and had great legs. She was intelligent, talented, and funny. She sang; she danced. She was perfect for the Broadway musical stage. Somewhere in the middle of the summer, she was preparing to star in one of the Green Mansions shows.

The night of the show, I sneaked into the Green Mansions owner's garden and picked a huge bouquet of flowers and presented them to Lois after her performance. She was so taken by my gesture that we spent the night together. It was the start of a love affair that lasted a lifetime. Even though we went our separate ways, we always stayed in touch.

Through the rest of the summer, I juggled my time between Nancy and Lois. It got complicated because we all lived and worked at the resort. It was stressful but exciting. At the end of summer, I continued seeing both Nancy and Lois in New York. Nancy lived on the Lower East Side. Lois lived on the Upper West Side. Nancy was attending New York University.

Lois was going on auditions during the day and performing at night at Upstairs at the Duplex in the village, a well-known club where young comedians and singers worked to get exposure. Lois would do her act, along with up-and-coming stars like Joan Rivers,

Rodney Dangerfield, Jo Anne Worley. On the nights when I wasn't with Nancy, I would go to the track and then head down to the village to catch Lois's last set. When I showed up backstage, Jo Anne Worley and Joan Rivers would refer to me as "Lois's trick." "Hey, Lois, your trick is here," they would shout.

Lois referred to me as "the Bronx Bastard." I don't know which is worse, being called Lois's trick or the Bronx Bastard. Doesn't matter. We were having a good time. Everything at this point in my life was going along well. Seeing Nancy and Lois at the same time presented no problems, so why change anything? *What's next?*

Enter Ronnie Ruggles, Followed
by Lenny the Lock

One afternoon, I was in a poker game and won some money. Nothing significant. Around five o'clock, I decided to call it a day, take my winnings, and leave the game. One of the guys I had just met at the poker game asked where I was going. I told him I wanted to go down to see the game at Madison Square Garden that night and was stopping at the bookmaker to place a bet. "Sounds great," he said. "I'd like to go along with you."

"Sure, by the way my name is Bobby Ochs."

"I'm Ronnie Ruggles," he replied.

Off we went. Ronnie and I each won our bets that night. That led to our becoming fast friends, gambling partners, and roommates.

Ronnie worked as a paper hanger, but he was as big a gambling junkie as I was. We bet on anything and everything. My bookie was Sydney, who owned and worked out of a pizzeria on Macombs Road. It was a more sophisticated operation for taking bets than the Sugar Bowl. You were given a phone number to call in your bets, and you settled up at the end of the week. Sydney was a bookie and knew me well enough not to give me a credit line. So I brought in Ronnie Ruggles and pitched him as a wealthy kid.

Ronnie showed up in a classy-looking sweater, and I introduced them. Funny that they would take my word and give Ronnie a credit line when he would not to give me a credit line. Anyway, my vouching for Ronnie got him a credit line of six hundred dollars, not shabby in 1963.

Ronnie's first bet with his new line of credit was on the Yankees. The Yankees were on a roll. Ronnie laid six hundred dollars to win five hundred bucks, and they took his bet. But it was one of those nights, and the Bronx Bombers bombed, and Ronnie suddenly had to get out of town. Both of us were broke, and we were in big, big trouble.

I had a friend, Billy Eisenberg, whose father owned a hotel in Lenox, Massachusetts. Right after the game, I called him and told him that I was sending my friend Ronnie to spend the summer up there. "Put him to work," I said.

Ronnie went home and packed his bags, and I got him on the next bus to Lenox, where he spent the summer. I stayed in New York to take the heat. Luckily, the goons didn't beat me up, but Ronnie and I knew we had to make good with the bookmakers. At summer's end and Ronnie back in the Bronx, we met with Cicero, one of the guys who worked for Sydney, in the lobby of the building where Ronnie's parents lived. Cicero came with a couple of goons. This wasn't going to be easy. However, it was clear we weren't going to mess with these guys, and we made a deal to pay them the following week.

We were at the racetrack almost every night. When we were winning, we would press our bets just raising how much money we bet; that got our juices flowing. True gamblers pushing the limits, you have to be in action and feel the excitement. At Yonkers, we got a reputation as being high rollers, big bettors, and attracted a lot of seedy characters. Among them was Lenny the Lock, a kid from Brooklyn who worked in the stables and the paddock cleaning up. Every night, Lenny the Lock approached Ronnie and me with a hot tip he had heard from a trainer or driver. "This horse here in the fifth race can't lose," he would say and always added, "It's a mortal lock." Every horse he touted was always "a lock"—hence, Lenny the Lock.

On the nights Ronnie and I were doing good at the track, we would throw Lenny a five or ten spot. After all, you never know. Besides he was entertaining and worth ten dollars to get a laugh. One night, he had some interesting information to share with us. He told us his friend Steve Casanova was working as an assistant trainer to one of the driver-trainers. Lenny goes on to tell us that Steve was training a horse at Freehold Raceway in New Jersey and that the horse was being primed to win and was shipped up to Roosevelt Raceway. He also told us that Steve just got married and didn't have money to bet the horses because the driver-trainer didn't pay much to his assistant trainers. So Steve was looking for somebody to make a bet for him in exchange for his information.

Ronnie and I looked at each other and said in unison, "We're your guys. Tell your friend Steve we'd like to meet him."

A few days later, Lenny tells us Steve Casanova would meet us before the first race at Roosevelt Raceway in two days. We told him we'd be there. The only problem was that on the day of the meeting, Ronnie and I went bust after a bad losing streak and had twenty dollars between us. "What the hell," we said and decided to go to the track to meet this Casanova guy. There was nothing to lose.

When we got to the track before the first race, there was no sign of Lenny the Lock and his friend Steve. Now Ronnie and I, two losers at the track with fourteen dollars between us after deducting the expense of getting to the track, figure there is only one thing to do. We bet our last fourteen dollars on a cold daily double. We picked one horse in the first race and coupled it with a horse in the second race—a two-horse parley, a true sucker bet.

In order to win, both horses have to win. Meanwhile, still no sign of Lenny and Steve. The first race goes off. We win it. We look at the tote board, which shows the payoff of the daily double possibilities, and we see that the horse we picked to win the second race would pay two hundred dollars for a two-dollar bet. So the fourteen dollars we bet stood to collect us over 1,400 dollars.

The second race was about to begin when Lenny and Steve show up. Lenny introduces us to Steve. The race is about to start, and I tell them to sit down. Ronnie and I sat stunned as the horse we picked crossed the finish line first. As much as we wanted to jump up and down and scream, we played it cool, like it's no big deal. Happens all the time. I tell Steve to come with us while we collect. Steve and Lenny stand next to us as the cashier peels off 1,400 dollars and hands it to me. I put it into my empty pocket. Steve, seeing this, now knows that Lenny brought him to the right guys, and Steve gives us his inside information.

The horse's name is Four Oaks Lady. The trainer-driver of the horse managed to hold the horse back while racing in Freehold, so when he shipped Four Oaks Lady to Roosevelt Raceway, the horse was classified three grades below the horses she should be racing against. Four Oaks Lady, an A horse, was entered in a race against C horses. A horses generally can run about four seconds faster than any C horse in a mile race. Steve also said that the trainer-driver planned to bet five hundred dollars of his own money, which was a big thing because he had a reputation around the track as being very tight, and a five-hundred-dollar bet on a race was like Jack Benny making that bet.

Steve also told us that he had been seen working the horse and was sure that Four Oaks Lady was in top shape and should kill the field she was racing against. He tells us the horse will be in the second race at Roosevelt in three nights. Ronnie and I were sold. I told Steve that if the horse wins, we would give him ten percent of our winnings and told him to meet us the night of the race before it began. I wanted last-minute confirmation that everything's a go before we bet. He was fine with the whole setup.

The night of the race Steve, Ronnie, and I met at Gam Wah Chinese Restaurant two hours before the track opened. While near the track, Gam Wah's reputation for good food was zero, so it was a good spot if we didn't want anyone seeing us. Steve told us it was a full go, and the driver was definitely betting five hundred dollars. I told Steve that if the horse wins, we would meet him after the race to give him his cut at the diner near the track. You didn't need to know which diner. Everyone met there for the sunny side eggs served in the pan they were cooked in.

Ronnie and I decided to bet our whole bankroll that night, which was close to the 1,400 dollars we won when we first met Steve. The race went off, and Four Oaks Lady wins by five lengths. No contest. The race went exactly as Steve said it would. We won six thousand dollars and met Steve to give him his six-hundred-dollar share. Steve, a kid who basically cleaned up horse manure, just got married. This was huge for him.

As we are eating the house special sunny side eggs, I offered Steve a proposition. As long as he delivers winning information, we will bet for him. I tell him he won't have to go into his pocket, that whatever we win, he would get ten percent. However, if we lose, his ten percent of our bet would come off the next winner. He loved it. "I'm in," he said. A deal was born.

Four Oaks Lady kept winning in the following two weeks even though she was moved up in class. Each time, we cashed big bets. While Ronnie and I were up about thirty thousand dollars, we knew we couldn't rely on Four Oaks Lady to keep winning, especially since she kept being moved up in class. We had to expand our operation.

Steve Casanova's information was limited to one horse. However, we realized that he could have access to other drivers and trainers. Steve was known and liked among the horsemen and could move freely in the paddock, which was where the horses and drivers gathered before they entered the track. Someone like Steve could get last-minute information as to what might happen in a race that was just about to be run.

The problem was that the paddock was located on the opposite side of the stands from where the betting windows were, so even if you heard that a certain driver felt very good about a horse's chances to win, you couldn't get to the windows in time to place a bet. Knowing this, Ronnie and I convinced Steve that he had to be in the paddock every night for every race. We set up a series of signals: hand in right pocket meant the 1 horse, hand in left pocket meant the 2 horse, arms crossed meant the 3 horse, and so went the signals. The three of us rehearsed the signals over and over so there would be no mistakes. I made it clear to Steve that we only wanted to bet horses he had complete confidence would win. While that wouldn't guarantee a horse would win, it would give us a huge edge.

Ronnie and I went out and bought a high-power pair of binoculars to see Steve's signals. We put the plan in place, and it was working great. Within a month's time, we ran our bankroll up to one hundred thousand dollars, a not-too-shabby score back in the mid-1960s.

The only problem was that it was turning into being a job. It became work. Ronnie and I had to show up at the track every night and sit there in cold weather with binoculars looking for a signal. Most of the time, we wouldn't get a signal from Steve if he didn't hear anything worthwhile. So for me and Ronnie, two gamblers at heart, sitting all night at the track and not making a bet was not what we wanted. On the nights we won, it was great, but it was work we weren't looking for.

When we started, Ronnie and I agreed that we would show some discipline and bet only the horses that we got from Steve. In business, that principle makes sense, but for guys who want action, it's just a job punching the clock. Even buying another pair of even more high-powered, expensive binoculars didn't make seeing signals any better. So we strayed from our discipline plan and immediately started losing back the one hundred thousand dollars. The truth is Ronnie and I were getting on each other's nerves. Spending all our time together, not working, and not having fun got to be too much.

The night that things came to an end started as a typical night. We were sitting in the grandstands in Roosevelt Raceway. Not much action. No signals from Steve. Ronnie and I weren't talking to each other mostly because there was not much to say. We actually sat through most of the races without betting. In the last race, Steve signals us two horses. The number 1 horse was the favorite at eight to five. The number 8 horse was a long shot at twenty-five to one. We were getting excited.

It was an exacta race where you play two horses to come in first and second. So we bet two hundred dollars on the 1-8 combo and two hundred dollars on the 8-1 ticket. If the 1-8 won, we would collect about twenty-five thousand dollars for our two-hundred-dollar bet, and if 8-1 won, we would collect about sixty thousand dollars. Ronnie says to me, "Let's bet two thousand dollars on the 1 horse, which would net three thousand dollars, as a saver in case the 8 runs out."

I say, "Why not take a shot and bet two thousand dollars on the 8 at twenty-five to one, which would bring back fifty thousand dollars?"

We argued back and forth and decided not to bet either the 1 or the 8 straight and would stick to the exacta bets we had. As the race goes off, the 8 goes right to the front, the 1 is five lengths behind the 8, and the rest of the field is about two lengths behind the 1. They were running like this all the way around the track, and the 8 horse crosses the finish line five lengths ahead of the 1. The 1 horse is running down the stretch about to take second place, which would bring us sixty thousand dollars. Ronnie and I are screaming in victory. When the horse behind the 1 horse came out of the pack to nip the 1 horse in a photo finish. The 8 horse paid over fifty dollars for a two-dollar bet. Not only did we lose a sixty-thousand-dollar decision, we also lost a fifty-thousand-dollar one by not betting two thousand dollars on the 8 horse.

Looking back, I can't believe we didn't bet both the 1 horse and the 8 horse straight. That would have made sense. It's not that we didn't have the money to make the bet. Ronnie's argument to bet two thousand dollars on the 1 horse was that it handicapped better than the 8 horse. I argued back that Steve signaled us both horses, not indicating who would be the winner. I said we shouldn't be handicapping the race, and if we bet a saver, we should take a shot on the 8 horse at twenty-five to one. Hindsight's twenty-twenty.

We left the track without saying a word, got into the car, and took a long, silent trip back to the Bronx. We barely spoke to each other. Shortly after that, Ronnie got married and moved out of the Clarke Place apartment to Riverdale. I was still single and moved from Clarke Place to Fort Lee, New Jersey. Ronnie's marriage was short-lived. I moved into his Riverdale apartment. He went to live with a girlfriend in Manhattan. *So what's next?*

Enter Benny Fein, Back to Bartending, and Conrad Grieves

B enny Fein was one of the biggest bookmakers in New York. He had about thirty runners working for him. With my money running out and no job, I decided to take an offer Benny offered me. "Bobby, you know a lot of gamblers. Why don't you come work for me as a runner and develop your own sheet of players? The deal is I'll back you whatever you win for the week, and you get half. When you have a losing week, I will give you all the money to pay off your players until you start to win, then fifty percent comes off the top before you get your end."

I took the deal, and it didn't take me long to have a sheet with over twenty solid players. The main problem with this setup was that players played on credit. Here's how it worked: Benny had an office with about three or four guys taking bets on the phone. I gave my clients their phone number and a code authorizing them to bet under my name. I had to establish a credit line for each player. Once a player went over his line of credit in a week, I would have to okay him if he wanted to place a bet. The week ended on Sunday, and on Monday, you had to settle with your players—pay some, collect from others. Benny knew only one thing: if my sheet lost, he gave me the amount to pay off. However, if my sheet made money, I would be held responsible for that money—no excuses.

Monday morning would come. If I had a good week, I would get a call from Benny at seven in the morning, waking me up. He would say, "Good week: 2,500 dollars due. Go get it." Even though the guys I had on my sheet were working or had businesses, they were married with kids, which made the job of collecting a struggle. "I'm a little short this week. Catch you in a couple of days," were the buzzwords, and I was always juggling a lot of money every week, collecting and paying Benny. Not much was coming to me. I needed a steady income along with taking book. I needed a job.

Conrad Grieves, the man who taught me how to be a bartender at the Stadium Motor Lounge, had opened Conrad's Cloud Room, which was a very successful nightclub in a motel in Queens near LaGuardia Airport. He knew I was looking for work and offered me a job as a bartender. I started right away. The club was always busy, busy enough to keep three bartenders pumping drinks all night seven days a week. Between bartending and running for Benny, the bucks were flowing in. Working at Conrad's was very, very lucrative, but I quickly realized that just about every wise guy and wannabe wise guy were coming in every night, which made me uncomfortable.

One night, when I was working behind the bar with the two other bartenders, Dickie Cantor and Bobby Grimaldi, three guys walked in and asked for Conrad. Conrad was off that night, so they grabbed Gene Miller, who was the host-manager. Two of the thugs started smacking him around. The third guy came over to the bar, sat down, and loudly whispered to me, Dickie, and Bobby. "Look at my hand," he said, holding a gun with a napkin over it. "You see this?"— pointing to the gun. "Now you guys stay nice and still."

The place was busy, and the music was loud, so it took a few seconds for the customers to realize that a couple of guys were beating the hell out of the manager. A regular customer ran over to help. The two guys dropped the manager to the floor with a couple of blows to his head and then turned on the customer. Within seconds, the poor guy was a bloody mess, an inch from death. Everyone in the club froze as the guy holding the gun on me and the other two bartenders raised the gun in the air as the three thugs walked out as if nothing happened.

The message was loud and clear from the wise guys who controlled Queens. They were out to take over Conrad's nightclub. Although I was shaken, I came to work the next night. The two other bartenders and I were behind the bar, and we were uneasy and still jittery from the night before when we noticed a very large man sitting very quietly by himself, having a drink. He got up from his barstool and walked to the middle of the dance floor, pulled out a pistol, and fired off three rounds into the wall near the front door. I immediately hit the deck.

As people were screaming and scrambling, the very large gunman calmly exited the club. Second message to Conrad. Luckily, nobody was hurt that night, but it was high alert for Conrad.

I'd had it. I went over to Conrad that night and told him I was through and that he should sell the club and leave town. However, Conrad, a Black man from Barbados, was living his dream and making tons of money and owning fancy cars. He had a wife, kids, and a blond white girlfriend. He didn't get it, and he wasn't about to leave the good life he made for himself. Me? I was out of there, leaving a very lucrative job. The signs were too clear to ignore. Luckily, I still had my sheet with Benny and was alive.

With lots of pride and no smarts for the underworld, Conrad went on to name the biggest crime boss in Queens as the guy muscling in on his nightclub. The district attorney got the grand jury to indict the mobster and had him placed under arrest. While he could easily have put up bail, he chose to stay in jail to wait for trial. Unlike Conrad, he knew how to stay alive.

While the alleged crime boss was in jail under police supervision, Conrad kept working his busy nightclub. One night, Bobby, the bartender who always idolized wise guys, went to Conrad and told him that someone wanted to talk to him. He led Conrad to the street. There were two men with guns. They opened fire, killing Conrad as he ran down the street. With Conrad, the key witness, dead and the mob boss safely behind bars, the mob boss was let go, set free. A waitress who worked in the motel coffee shop had identified the killers. The trial was a joke. The two murderers were tried for killing Conrad. Bobby the bartender was being tried as an accomplice. The waitress who witnessed the killing changed her story. She also knew how to stay alive. The killers walked. Only the poor schmuck of a bartender served six years in the can. And Conrad was dead.

Back to Benny's World

Bookmaking made it possible for Benny to live largely—big house in exclusive Pelham Manor, married to a beautiful, high-maintenance wife who liked her fancy cars, furs, and expensive summers in mountain resorts. They had three children, two daughters and a son. This was a far cry for Benny, who grew up in the Depression when he'd have to sleep at the doorsteps of his betting clients so they'd trip over him and have to pay up.

While Benny's gambling operation adequately supported his lifestyle, he had to justify living large and show legitimate earnings, so he bought a plastics manufacturing company to show legitimate income and to give his son Steven a business to run. The plastics company office was laid out so that Steve had one office in the factory that made plastic bags for commercial use, and Benny sat in the next office, where he conducted his bookie operation.

Steve was twenty-five, married with a couple of kids, and living in Great Neck. He worked but didn't make big bucks. He was going through a divorce, and he took an apartment in Manhattan. I was single. We started hanging out together. He liked playing the horses and sports betting. When he wanted to get a bet down, he would play on my sheet and use a fictitious name so his father wouldn't know that he was gambling. I would say to him, "What are you, crazy, Steve? If you need money, just ask your father. Why are you betting?" I knew the answer. It wasn't the money. It was the action he wanted, and he didn't want his father knowing he was gambling.

I used to laugh to myself on the days I would go to the factory to pick up money from Steve for a bet he lost. I'd get the money from Steve and go to the next office to give Benny the money or vice versa. It was a trip. When Steve and I were hanging out together and Benny asked me to keep an eye on Steve to see that he didn't get in trouble, that gave me another laugh. Okay, so I wouldn't let Steve get into any trouble. Right, like I could or would be able to stop him, but Steve and I did run up high bills on Steve's credit card. We dined at the best restaurants, went nightclubbing every night, and made regular trips to the track. That was my idea of keeping Benny's son out of trouble.

One Friday, Steve tells me that he met a sexy girl, really stacked, at one of his accounts, a men's sock manufacturer in the garment center. He said she was the boss' secretary and single. "That sounds great. When are you going to take her out?" I asked.

Steve, who was dating someone else at the time, said, "I'm not, but you should." He gave me her name and number.

Carolyn Atlas. Why not? I thought. A nine-to-five, Monday-to-Friday working girl would be a far cry from the cocktail waitresses who worked all night. I figured I'd give her a call.

It was around five o'clock and got Carolyn on the phone. I introduced myself and told her, "Steve Fein was a friend of mine, and he thought you and I should get together. How about tonight? I can pick you up around seven."

Carolyn, in a sweet, very sexy voice, said, "You're calling me up at five o'clock on a Friday to ask me out tonight? I don't think so."

I asked if she was busy. She said she wasn't. "So you are choosing to stay home on principle rather than having dinner with me?" I asked.

She paused and said okay. I arrived at her apartment building on Seventy-Eighth and Third at seven o'clock and rang the bell. The door opened, and there stood a beautiful, well-endowed young woman named Carolyn Atlas. The rest is history, and *what's next?*

Enter Carolyn

We went to a restaurant where I had to collect money from the manager who played on my Benny Fein sheet. While Carolyn and I were dining, when she finished her shrimp cocktail, I told the waiter, "Please bring the lady another shrimp cocktail." Why I remember that, I don't know, but I realized that Steve hadn't told her what I did for a living. She had no idea.

Later in our relationship, she told me she thought I might be a doctor when she saw the wad of hundreds I pulled out to pay the bill. Wishful thinking on the part of a single young Jewish girl from Long Island. Normally, it didn't take me more than the second date, if not the first night, to make it to bed with a date. But I wasn't going to score with Carolyn that night. When we got back to her apartment building, she said she had a great time, and yes, she would like to see me again and good night.

This was different. We started dating regularly. I enjoyed her company and liked talking to her, and yes, I wanted to score. But scoring with Carolyn was a waiting game. For a while, it was dinner at restaurants and ending the evening at her apartment, playing gin rummy. It wasn't long before we got it on, and it was worth the wait.

I was living in Riverdale at the time, so Carolyn and I spent a lot of time in each other's apartment. She was great and didn't seem bothered by my gambling. However, her breaking point came the weekend of college football bowl games during the Christmas holidays when there was one game after another on TV that weekend, and I had a lot of betting action the whole time. The players on my sheet were going crazy, betting big and betting just about every game. My plan for that weekend with Carolyn was to stay in bed, screw, order in, and watch every game.

She was a trooper Friday night and all day Saturday. Sunday, we were still in bed with empty containers of Chinese food, empty pizza boxes, and half-eaten corned beef sandwiches. I could tell that Carolyn was going to snap. Sometime between games and after lying in bed for three days, she screamed, "We got to get out of here—anywhere! This is too much. A movie, any movie. Just let's get out of here!"

Off we went to a steak house for dinner and a movie. Things were going great. I loved being around Carolyn. I was making money with Benny. I didn't know it, but it was the quiet before the storm.

Nightfall

One morning, after spending the night with Carolyn at her apartment on Seventy-Eighth Street, I drove to my apartment building in Riverdale. As I was getting out of my car, I was met by two FBI agents. They approached me, saying, "Robert Ochs, you are under arrest," handcuffed me, put me into their car, and took me to FBI headquarters on Sixty-Sixth Street and Third Avenue, where they placed me in a large pen.

I couldn't believe it! It was like old home week. Benny and his entire crew of runners were there and also under arrest. Benny came over to me and said, "Don't worry. We'll be out sometime today. My lawyer will be here to get us out."

For Benny, an old pro, this was routine. He had been arrested many, many times. He started taking book back in the early '30s during the Depression. Me? I was in my twenties, nervous and scared about what was going to happen. The prospect of doing time was a big deal to me. It couldn't happen.

Later that day, we were all transferred to the courthouse in downtown Manhattan to be arraigned. We were sitting in front of the judge when Benny's lawyer Max Fruchman walked into the courtroom and approached the judge's bench. Max looked like he was out of central casting for lawyers. Probably in his sixties, he had a full head of perfectly coiffed silver hair. He was tanned and wearing a thousand-dollar suit. A Melvin Belli type, Max sure knew his way around the courtroom.

After approaching the judge, we were all released on our own recognizance and charged with operating an illegal gambling operation, which was a federal offense. We would be going to trial in several months before Judge Lee Gagliardi.

Turns out the FBI was investigating Benny's operation for months, and all of our phones were tapped. There were photos of us making bets, talking to witnesses. There was no way out. We were going to be found guilty as charged.

The months leading up to the trial were excruciating. I could go to jail for who knew how long. I moved in with Carolyn in her apartment. She was very supportive and gave me great comfort during those very tough days.

On the day of the trial, on advice of Fruchman, I pled guilty, hoping for a light sentence. After Fruchman's argument, Judge Gagliardi lectured me on the values of the straight and narrow and then sentenced me to two years' probation. No jail time, but I would have to report to a probation officer once a month for the next two years. And forever after, I would have a record as a "KG," meaning that I was a "known gambler." When I think back to my being branded KG, I can't help but compare it to how gambling is viewed today. Sports betting is alive and kicking, and the government gets a cut and advertises on every manner of all media 24-7.

What a relief! No jail time! A ton of bricks was lifted off my back. Benny and a few of the guys who handled the phone were sentenced to six months of prison time in Connecticut. This meant nothing to Benny. He was taking bets on the hall phone outside the courtroom before appearing before the judge. While doing his six months, he was conducting business from jail. For Benny, it was a change of office venue. For me, it was over. I was lucky not having to do time. *So what's next?*

Bye-Bye, Benny; Hello Legit Life

L iving with Carolyn was a major stabilizing point in my life. Without her, I knew I would have been tempted to go back to my old ways with Benny. I didn't want to lose Carolyn. I started working as a bartender at watering holes in Manhattan. First, there was Skitch Henderson's Daly's Daffodil. Skitch was a well-known orchestra leader who appeared on *Tonight Starring Steve Allen*. Carolyn was Skitch's private secretary until he went to jail, something to do with taxes.

I worked a bunch of other popular spots: Rick Newman's Catch a Rising Star; Slate's steak house on West Fifty-Seventh Street next to CBS Studios, where CBS personalities ate and drank; and several bars along First Avenue when First Avenue was a hot spot for singles.

One of the places I worked at was Michael's Pub, which was owned by Gil Wiest. Gil was quite a character. He hired me to manage the pub where well-known entertainers performed. At that time, Woody Allen was making movies and doing stand-up. He also played clarinet in a Dixieland band, and Gil booked Woody's eight-piece band for Monday nights for several months and placed ads in newspapers and magazines to publicize that Woody Allen would be appearing on Monday nights. And every Monday night, the place was sold out with lines out the door. Everybody wanted to see Woody Allen.

Woody, however, always wore his army fatigue jacket and a hat that covered his face. While on stage, he sat along and played as part of the band, and as soon as the set was over, he would leave. The audience was eating and drinking and never realized that Woody was in the band that had just played. They expected Woody would be doing his comedy act. When they asked me, "When does Woody go on?" I would tell them that he was part of the band that had just played. This meant that every Monday, I was close to being lynched. Gil Wiest thought nothing of it.

Trying to Unseat Michel LeGrand

M ichael's Pub sat 150 with a bandstand. All the tables were covered with white tablecloths, except for three tables in front of the bandstand. Those tables had oakwood tops and were held exclusively for VIP guests and whoever Gil said was a VIP. One night, before Gil arrived, Michel LeGrand, the famous musical composer, including the cast of *The Umbrellas of Cherbourg*, came in with a party of six. I immediately took LeGrand and his party to the VIP table.

When Gil arrived and saw people sitting at a VIP table without his prior approval, he told me, "Get them off that table *now*." I said that Michel LeGrand was the VIP and that they were in the middle of eating dinner. Gil screamed that he didn't care and that he was the only one who can seat anyone at a VIP table and to move them to another table. I went over to LeGrand's table and said that I was sorry, but I had to move him to a different table.

He looked at me stunned and said nothing. No response. I thought maybe since he is French, he didn't understand me. I asked him if he understood English. In perfect English, he said, "Yes, I do. Now leave us alone."

I did. My days at Michael's Pub were numbered. Gil continued advertising Woody's appearances despite complaints of fraud, and I couldn't abide his irrational seating tactics and quit.

During this time, I asked Carolyn to marry me. She wasn't too quick to say yes. I mean, why wouldn't she jump at marrying a bartender, a philanderer with a criminal KG record. But she succumbed, and we set the date for October 14, 1973. The ceremony was at the Furrier Union Temple on West Twenty-Sixth Street. We chose it because Carolyn's father, who passed away the year before, was one of the union's founders. After the union rabbi married us, all 150 of us went uptown to Tavern on the Green in Central Park for the reception.

It was a beautiful affair on a glorious October Sunday afternoon—cocktails in the garden, an elaborate buffet lunch, dancing to a six-piece band. Carolyn's mother Evelyn made sure that her only daughter would have the wedding of every girl's dream. Carolyn looked beautiful. I was a pretty good-looking groom, if I must say so myself.

Life after Marriage

Now came the honeymoon. Being short on cash, I called Izzy Snow to help out. Yep, the same Izzy Snow who owned the College Rec Pool Room of my youth and my sometime bookie and the same Izzy Snow who made the aborted arrangements for me to marry Linda Bushn in Las Vegas ten years earlier. Izzy was now running junkets to casinos and a crap game on the second floor over Bruno's Italian Restaurant on East Fifty-Eighth Street. Izzy got us a junket to Curacao, an island just off Venezuela. The deal was that as long as I did some gambling at the casino, everything would be comped.

Carolyn and I invited Milty Cohen and his wife, Sharon, to join us on our honeymoon. Why not? Carolyn and I were together for so long that having Milty and Sharon join us would be great fun. Milty was the best man at our wedding, and Milty and I spent our teen years and beyond in Izzy Snow's College Rec Pool Room

Milty, Sharon, Carolyn, and I boarded the plane to Curacao for four days of fun and sun, all comped, on a tropical island. Like Izzy told me, if I played a little at the crap table and showed my face every night in the casino, everything would be comped.

We got to the hotel in the early afternoon. The rooms were fine. We unpacked and spent some time on the beach, then dinner in the hotel restaurant, and off to show our faces and do some gambling in the casino.

My plan was to bet small and not lose too much and maybe get lucky and win some, but a few things took me by surprise. When I got to the crap table to roll the dice and tried to make a ten-dollar bet on the pass line, I found that there was a twenty-five-dollar-minimum bet. I didn't plan on that, but okay. So I changed my bet to twenty-five dollars and quickly noticed that the odds on making your point was less than the odds you got in Vegas, Puerto Rico, or even a back alley in the Bronx.

I immediately questioned the pit boss who said that those were the house rules, take it or leave it. I told Milty and our wives that this was bullshit and we're getting out of here. I called Izzy. He said he wasn't aware of what was going on down there. I told him to get us out of there. "I'll take care of it and call you back in an hour," he said.

An hour later, Izzy called and said he booked a flight for the four of us to Puerto Rico and reserved two rooms at the El San Juan Hotel. "Everything will be taken care of. Be at the airport tomorrow at noon. You'll have a private plane."

I hung up and told my gang to pack. We were taking off the next morning for Puerto Rico. When we got to the hotel checkout the next morning, we got a bill, not only for the rooms and food for the days we were there but for the three nights that we weren't going to be there. I told them I wasn't paying for time we weren't there, that we were there on Izzy Snow's junket, and everything was comped. The cashier called the manager, saying, "I'm sure he will straighten everything out."

The next thing I know, two goons approached us in the hotel lobby. "What seems to be the problem?" asked one of them. I told him. He nodded and said, "I understand you just got married and this was supposed to be your honeymoon. It would be a shame if your wife had to go back to New York a widow." Message heard loud and clear.

Milty and I went into a huddle and came up with the cash to cover the bill. We were happy to get out of there alive, but when we got to the airport and saw the plane taking us to Puerto Rico, we weren't too sure about how much longer we had. It was a single-engine plane that looked like it was powered by a rubber band and sat four plus the pilot's and copilot's seats, except there was no copilot, and the pilot looked like he'd been flying with the Wright brothers.

Milty, Sharon, Carolyn, and I stepped nervously into this jalopy of a plane. The pilot assured us that we'd be fine. "I made this trip many times," he assured us. We took off and, for the length of the trip, were flying low over the ocean. Carolyn and I clung to each other, so did Milty and Sharon. We landed safely and got to the hotel in one piece. What a way to start a marriage, an omen of things to come: exciting, eventful, rocky, and knowing that Carolyn and I would cling to each other and get through it all together.

Honeymoon Over, Family Life Awaits

B ack from our honeymoon and back to Carolyn's one-bedroom apartment on Seventy-Eighth Street with its small kitchen and working fireplace, where we were starting out as newlyweds, although we had been living together for almost three years and been through a lot. After several years of bartending, Carolyn's brother Bob Atlas talked to me about working for him and his partner in art liquidation sales. Bob had been doing this for some time.

Bartending had run its course for me. I was making just enough to pay the bills and decided to give Bob's offer a try. The way it worked was that Bob would buy commercial paintings imported from China, where they were manufactured by machine or by a factory of low-wage painters who knocked them off by the thousands. Once the paintings were put in a frame, they looked good hanging on a wall. Bob would buy a truckload of these affordable paintings and frames, rent a banquet hall in an out-of-town hotel, and place an ad in the local paper about the weekend liquidation art sale that would be taking place on Saturday and Sunday only.

Because he was able to buy the goods very cheap, he sold them very cheap. So people who wanted to decorate their home and couldn't afford to go to a gallery could buy attractive, inexpensive art. It was perfect for them. We would sell these paintings nonstop all day long all weekend. It was an okay business for Bob and his partner. I was getting a salary, just enough to cover my bills. After a while, with Bob's blessing, I decided to go off on my own doing art sales.

What I needed to start was ten thousand dollars' worth of inventory and cash to cover the rental of a hotel room, advertising, and truck rental. I didn't have the first dollar and passed the business plan to Milty. He put up the cash, and we were in business and started out doing very well, so well that Milty got his initial investment back within several months.

Working with Milty was great. It didn't seem like working a job. Our week started on Monday. We followed the routine I learned working with my brother-in-law: making calls to out-of-town hotels mostly in New Jersey and Connecticut. Once we booked a room, I would go to the local newspaper and place an ad to run on Friday. On Wednesday, we would drive to Long Island to purchase paintings and frames. On Friday, we rented a truck, loaded it, and drove to our destination to set up for the art show. On Saturday and Sunday, we would sell all day and be home Sunday night for dinner.

We did so well that we hired two young guys to load, drive the truck, and set up the show. Milty and I showed up on Saturday to work the show and collect the cash. Most of the time, Carolyn and Sharon would join us. It made for perfect great weekends and was profitable,

Life was good: out of town; hotel rooms; breakfast, lunch, and dinners all weekend; and best of all, the cash was coming in, not get-rich money but enough to justify my not working for anyone. Being my own boss and not having to answer to anyone was my lifestyle. Milty and I did this for a couple of years, but like most good things, it came to an end. When word got out that there was money in art sales, we had competitors galore. It became more difficult to find locations and harder traveling to find locations. Expenses were higher. It wasn't lucrative to continue in art sales. Back to square one: working restaurants and bars. *What's next?*

Our wedding day—October 14, 1973

Carolyn & Bobby Ochs

Bobby, Carolyn & Samantha, East Hampton, NY, 1976

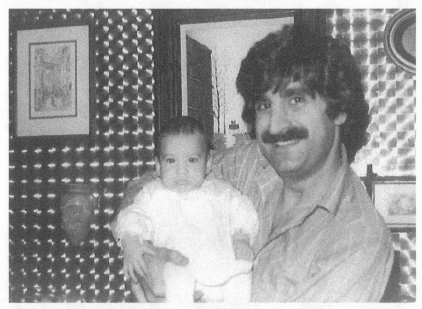

Samantha, four months old, January, 1976

Saint Martin, 1980

My family at Samantha's Bat Mitzvah

Carolyn, Samantha, Bobby

Carolyn, Bobby, & Samantha at Samantha Restaurant, 1980

Carolyn, Samantha, & Bobby, Park City, UT, 1993

Back to Bars, a Baby's Born

On September 5, 1975, a major event took place in Carolyn and my life that changed everything. We gave birth to a baby girl and named her Samantha Atlas Ochs. We took this little skinny, long thing back to our one-bedroom apartment on Seventy-Eighth Street. I knew things would have to change. I would have to make a normal life, have a stable job and income to take care of my family. With my background, it looked like restaurants and bars would have to be in my future.

For the next few years, I worked as a bartender but was just getting by and unable to save anything. By bartending, though, I developed a following, which would be helpful if I wanted to open a restaurant. However, without capital, it wasn't easy.

One day, as I left our apartment on Seventy-Eighth and Third, I was walking east. As I got to First and Seventy-Eighth, I noticed that the restaurant on the corner of Seventy-Eighth and First was closed and out of business. Bingo! A light went off in my head. The owners were two guys I knew. I first met them years ago when I was a kid hanging out at the College Rec Pool Room. Joey Childs and Shelly Shuster were Bronx guys and partners and wheeler dealers for years in buying, opening, and selling restaurants and bars. They were both about twelve years older than me and had a reputation on making deals all the time.

I called Joey and told him I had an idea for their closed restaurant. We met the next day in the restaurant. I proposed that we renovate and open a new place. Five different bars and restaurant were at that location and failed. They all featured pub food, mostly burgers. I told them that I wanted to make it a legitimate full-scale restaurant with a full menu I would create. Now I was making this proposal without any money and for a one-third partnership interest, and I would be the operating partner. They knew me and my reputation in the restaurant business and liked the idea. However, they said it would take about forty thousand dollars to fifty thousand dollars to renovate and start up. And they wanted to know if I had the money. I said I'd get back to them in a week.

Within a week, I convinced Carolyn to turn over five thousand dollars she had saved—squirreled away. It was the only money we had. Carolyn would say it was *her* money not *our* money. A couple of friends each loaned me 2,500 dollars for a total of ten thousand dollars.

Everybody I told that I was going to open a restaurant on the corner of Seventy-Eighth and First said I was crazy and warned that five restaurants failed in that location; it was jinxed. "You will never make it." I never listened to anyone's advice before, and I wasn't about to now. Joey, Shelly, and I agreed to each put up ten thousand dollars for a total of thirty thousand dollars to start the project. If needed— and it was—the vending company that supplied the jukebox and cigarette machine would give us ten thousand dollars. So with forty thousand dollars, we built and opened a new restaurant on May 7, 1978 and named it Samantha after my two-year-old daughter.

Most of the restaurants back then on the Upper East Side were basically pubs and featured hamburgers. The Samantha menu offered appetizers, entrees with a selection of seafood, chicken dishes (not a half-roasted chicken but chicken breast gismonda; stuffed chicken breast with chopped spinach, ricotta cheese, and parmesan cheese and rolled sautéed then baked topped with Mornay sauce), veal dishes, duck a l'orange. A lot of prep work was required, and we didn't have a chef and kitchen staff. The kitchen, by the way, was no bigger than an old-fashioned phone booth. The basement had a walk-in box and space to prep in.

The restaurant sat seventy; the bar sat fifteen. My work was cut out for me. Joey and Shelly left the entire operation for me to run as

I saw fit. They had other businesses and ventures, and I was in charge of all aspects of Samantha from creating the concept, design, and construction to hiring and training staff to public relations and marketing. Throughout the renovation period—which included adding an enclosed café, new floors, new ceiling, new fixtures, and upgrading kitchen equipment—I noticed an old Chinese man outside the restaurant on the sidewalk always leaning against a parked car. He was there every day. He smoked one cigarette after another.

One day, when we were about three weeks to completion, I needed someone other than myself to move tables and chairs and to start to clean up after construction. I went outside and approached the old chain-smoking gentleman and asked if he wanted to work. He grunted and shook his head yes. "You can call me Bobby. What do I call you?" I asked.

He grunted, "Chang."

I said, "Chang—that's it?"

He nodded yes.

"Okay, Mr. Chang."

Without my saying a word, Mr. Chang started arranging and cleaning nonstop the whole day. He never said a word, never asked what he would get paid, didn't ask if this was a permanent job—nothing. He just did everything without any instructions. At the end of the day, I asked him if he wanted a job. He nodded yes and showed up the next morning in the restaurant, not outside this time.

During the renovation, I was interviewing to hire staff. I hired a chef who seemed to have the right experience. He had worked in good kitchens. I tested him on the menu, and he produced the dishes the way I wanted them. He seemed to be okay with a small kitchen, and he recommended a sous-chef. Everything appeared to be fine when I talked to him. I hired him and the sous-chef. Mr. Chang would be the dishwasher, prep helper, and general maintenance man who would clean the restaurant after closing.

I put an ad in *Variety* for waitresses in the days before they were called servers or waitstaff. *Variety* was the trade paper where actors and actresses looked for audition information. Over four days, I probably interviewed about 150 aspiring young actresses to work as servers, taking notes on three-by-five index cards. When an interview was over, I indicated by code the appearance of the applicant and called twenty to tell them they got the job and to come in for training the following day. This is a practice that could and would never be used today. At that time, twenty very attractive brunettes showed up, all about five feet eight inches. They all looked alike, except for one who was blond and much shorter than the rest. She clearly stood out. Didn't matter. She was my niece.

The waitresses that I hired back in 1978 to work as servers to open Samantha Restaurant are a close-knit group to this day. Throughout the years and as of today, the original waitstaff stay in touch with each other and sometimes with me. They have a private Facebook page they call the Samantha Girls. One of those original Samantha Girls, Robin Reinhardt, stayed in regular touch with me, keeping me up-to-date about all the girls, what they were doing, and where they were living. Robin and a few of the girls, after working at Samantha's for about five years, moved to Los Angeles to pursue their acting careers. So it was Robin who would contact me with annual reports as to how everyone was doing. This went on for over thirty years.

One day, several years ago, I was alone in my Florida apartment aimlessly channel surfing on the TV when I came across the movie *Splash* starring Tom Hanks and Daryl Hannah. Robin was an extra in that movie, so as I watched the movie and realized I hadn't heard from Robin in some time, I decided to call her at her home in Los Angeles. Her husband, Kevin, whom I knew, answered. He was uncharacteristically uncomfortable as we chatted. Jokingly, I said, "Kevin, I just watched Robin in her award-winning performance in *Splash* and thought of her. How are you guys doing? Can I speak to Robin?"

Nervously, Kevin said, "It's not a good time for her to talk." He went on to say that he didn't want to tell anyone that Robin is suffering from dementia. "I don't think she should talk to anyone right now."

What? I thought. I couldn't wrap my brain around it. Shaken, I told Kevin how sorry I was and wanted Robin to know she was in my prayers and that I was thinking of her and understood why he didn't want to put her on the phone.

The next morning, Kevin called, sobbing and saying, "Bobby, I should have let you talk to Robin when you called. She died last night. I'm so, so sorry I didn't let her talk to you."

Life's strange sometimes. Why did I find an old movie on TV that particular day to remind me of Robin, whom I hadn't had contact with in quite some time, and why did I decide to call on the day she died? I don't know why. It's just strange, very strange and sad.

As the operating partner-manager, it was my job to get everybody ready for opening night. The date was set. Ready or not, we are going to open. As we learn in life, not everything goes according to plan. Sure enough, the chef and sous-chef don't show up. They were to come in at twelve noon to prep for a seven-o'clock opening. They didn't show. I was frantically calling their phones. No answer.

A major catastrophe was unfolding on the day of the opening of the restaurant. No food. At seven thirty, the restaurant was full. I could have told people at the door that we were postponing the opening, but that would send a negative message. Instead, I announced to everyone that there was a slight hiccup, and everything was on the house, drinks and hors d'oeuvres. Mr. Chang and Shelly cooked up spare ribs and chicken. I schmoozed the guests. It worked! Great public relations. People were talking about that night for months, but Samantha still needed a chef so it could stay open.

At the end of the night, I was sitting in the restaurant with a glass of scotch, trying to figure out my next move. Along comes Mr. Chang, grunting. Mr. Chang never talked. He just grunted. In incomprehensible English, he grunted, "Chef I got."

I say, "What are you talking about?"

"I bring chef in morning," he grunts.

In desperation, I say okay.

The next morning, Mr. Chang shows up with a Chinese man who looked to be in his thirties. He has a cheerful manner and appears to be self-assured. He says to me, "I'm your chef. Chang showed me the menu. No problem."

I ask him his name. He says to call him Cherry. I ask him, "Where do you work, and why do you think you can handle this menu?"

He names some restaurant where he works in a town in New Jersey. He then says again, "No problem."

I'm a desperate man, and desperate times call for desperate measures. "When can you start?" I ask.

"Right now," he says.

I tell him what I could pay.

Again, he says, "No problem."

Cherry and Chang immediately went to work taking inventory, making a list of items they needed, prepping, cleaning. They were amazing. Cherry executed the menu flawlessly. He was a one-man show with Chang his helper. He did all the prepping.

During service, he was on the line sautéing and grilling. Between Cherry and Mr. Chang, they managed to serve apps, entrées, and desserts to about one hundred guests a night. Each night, there were three nightly specials in addition to our regular menu: one seafood, one chicken, one veal. Cherry would butcher off a leg of veal.

Then came a prix fixe Sunday brunch: choice of Bloody Mary, mimosa, or screwdriver; a fresh fruit cup; choice of eggs Benedict, eggs Florentine, or three eggs any style; French toast, quiche Lorraine (made by Cherry), omelets, coffee or tea—all for 3.95 dollars. There were lines out the door from eleven in the morning to four in the late afternoon every Sunday. It was great public relations and marketing and turned out to be a huge moneymaker. As business grew, Cherry added some cooks to handle the volume, but Cherry was always there prepping and on the line.

I often wondered back then what if Mr. Chang didn't choose my restaurant to stake out. Neither Mr. Chang nor Cherry ever revealed if this was some sort of plan or just fate taking its course. Doesn't really matter. You make your own luck. But I wonder, what if there was no chain-smoking, grunting Mr. Chang? What would have been the outcome of Samantha Restaurant? *What's next?*

Samantha and Beyond

The building where Samantha Restaurant was located was in a rent-controlled five-story walk-up tenement. The woman who owned the building was a charming older Park Avenue woman who came to the restaurant every month to pick up the 1,350-dollar rent check. Her family always owned the building. On her monthly visits, we sat and had tea, and each time I told her, "When you want to sell your building, we would be interested in buying."

She always replied that the building was in her family for years, and she was going to give it to her son. "No sale. Thank you anyway."

For years I continued to ask if she would sell, and to my surprise, on one of her visits, she asked if I was still interested in buying the building. It seems her son didn't have the sentimental connection to the building she had. He wanted the money. We settled on a purchase price of 560,000 dollars with ten percent down (fifty-six thousand dollars) and monthly payments with interest at the then-current rate. Now we owned the building on the corner of First Avenue and Seventy-Eighth Street on the Upper East Side.

Samantha was still open, and Joey, Shelly, and I wanted to open other restaurants. People I knew were offering to invest in our next restaurant, and Joe, Shelly, and I were eager to take advantage of those offers. When we found a space in a prime location on Madison Avenue between Sixty-Third and Sixty-Fourth Street, we were in contact with Stuart Alpert and Seymour Alpert, who were successful real estate investors, and Bob Middleman, who was a lawyer. They agreed to invest with us in our next restaurant. We made the deal and built a one-hundred-seat restaurant with a bar that sat twenty and named it Marigold.

With Carolyn's help, we created a menu for Marigold. I was running back and forth between Samantha and Marigold. Shelly and Joey had been together and partners from back in the Bronx and were attached at the hip. When I disagreed with an issue with either one of them, I was instantly outvoted. With Samantha, there was generally no problem. Samantha was a success, so I was able to make most of the decisions and run the operation without any interference from them. At Marigold, however, Shelly and Joey wanted to be more involved.

On the one hand it was okay with me. I had enough to do. On the other hand, I didn't like Shelly's way of taking charge and found myself disagreeing with most of his decisions. But I was fighting a losing battle because Joey and Shelly acted as a unit. I realized that it would be detrimental to the business if Shelly and I were always in a disagreement. And it started to become a personal issue. Once Marigold was up and running and heading to being a profitable venture, I started to back off and gave Shelly the full control he wanted. I was content collecting an envelope with my share of the profits. Samantha was doing well. It was time to move on. *What's next?*

YOU ARE INVITED TO ATTEND
THE GRAND OPENING OF A NEW
EATING AND DRINKING ESTABLISHMENT

SAMANTHA

1495 First Ave. Cor. of 78 St.
New York, N.Y. 10021
Tel: (212) 744-9288

SUNDAY EVENING

MAY 7, 1978

7 P.M.

Invitation to the Grand Opening of Samantha

Samantha Restaurant

Bobby and Robin, circa 2000

The original "Samantha Girls"
Lucy, Debra, Betsey, Robin, and Janet

Hollywood Calls, Enter John Travolta

In the evening, I would come home late, sit at the kitchen table, light up a joint, turn on my tape recorder, and record stories of my growing up in the Bronx. Over a short period of time, I taped fifteen short stories, vignettes. Whoever listened to them found them interesting and humorous.

One day, Carolyn was reading Page Six in the *New York Post*. There was an item about my old girlfriend Lois Zetter from my Green Mansion days. She was managing Barry Bostwick, who was then starring in a Broadway musical. Carolyn showed me the article and said, "Why don't you call Lois?" How's that for a wife suggesting I should call an old girlfriend?

I hadn't had much contact with Lois for a while and thought it would be nice seeing and talking to her. It would be nice to catch up. I called, and we met for lunch at a midtown restaurant. For some reason, Lois could never land the role that would lead her to fame and fortune. She was the one who, if she was auditioning for a juicy role and two other actresses were trying out for the role, one of the others got the part. If Lois did get the part, the show would close the second night. She had the lead role in Broadway's *Hotel Passionata*. It closed the next day. That was Lois's career in a nutshell.

At one point, she even hired me to manage her career. The only job I got for her was singing at the Stadium Lounge, Arnie Rosen's joint. It lasted two nights. Done. So much for my career as an agent, and Lois, tired of doing Broadway productions on the road, decided to call it quits. She and Bob LeMond formed a partnership. LeMond was also an actor. They teamed up, and LeMond Zetter Management was born.

They took an office on Seventh Avenue and Fifty-Sixth Street next to the Carnegie Deli. At the time, they had no clients. With no clients and nobody knocking on their door, Bob suggested to Lois that they go see a friend of theirs who was starring in *Bye Bye Birdie* in a dinner theater somewhere in New Jersey. They went. While watching the production, LeMond noticed a chubby kid in the chorus, an extra, and told Lois to take a look at this kid. "There's something about him. I'm not sure, but I got a feeling."

After the show they went backstage to congratulate their friend, who was the star of the show. Bob sees the kid, introduces himself and Lois as talent managers. They hand him their business card and say, "If you're interested in pursuing a career, call us." The kid was fifteen and still in high school. He thanked Lois and Bob and left.

Some weeks later the kid called Bob and said he would like him and Lois to manage his career. Bob made an appointment for the kid and his mother to come to the office. A week or so later, they showed and signed a contract. Their first client, a fifteen-year-old chubby kid with no professional experience, except the one show at the dinner theater. Well, now they have a client, and what a client he turned out to be: John Travolta. Talk about hitting a home run your first time at bat!

As I was finishing my rare cheeseburger and Lois was digesting her Waldorf salad, I mentioned the tapes I'd recorded. She was very interested since she knew me in the days I was talking about on the tapes and told me that she was flying back to Los Angeles, where she and Bob had an office. Lois and LeMond had developed a very successful management company. "Send me the tapes. I would love to hear them," she said. We finished lunch and I promised to send them to her soon as possible.

As soon as she received the tapes, Lois called. She was very excited. She said she loved them and had John Travolta listen to them. He thought they were great, and she said he would be interested in playing me if it could be developed into a movie. Travolta just finished shooting *Urban Cowboy* and was looking for a new project. Lois told me to fly out to Los Angeles to meet Travolta and talk about developing a story line for a movie based on my life.

She asked me if I saw *Saturday Night Fever*. "Not only haven't I seen it, I never saw Travolta in anything, not even one episode of *Welcome Back, Kotter*," I told her. She said that I couldn't meet John without having seen his work. *Saturday Night Fever* wasn't playing any more in New York. It was about two years since its release.

She hung up and called me back an hour later to tell me that she set up a private screening for me at the Paramount Building on Broadway and Sixtieth Street to see *Saturday Night Fever* and wanted to know when I could see it. She said they will show it any time. "Five tomorrow evening works for me," I said.

The next day at five o'clock, I got to the Paramount, where I was greeted and shown to a small theater with maybe fifty seats. I was the only one there for a showing of *Saturday Night Fever*. A young lady asked if I wanted a drink. I declined, and she said, "Mr. Ochs, just let us know when you would like us to start the film." VIP treatment all the way. I thanked her and said to give me a minute.

After a moment, I nestled into the cushy seat and, in a loud voice, called out, "Okay, roll 'em!"

Lois Zetter had come a long way from Green Mansions and, with Bob LeMond, had major clout in Hollywood. In a fairly short time, LeMond-Zetter was handling Travolta and an impressive roster of A-list actors.

After viewing *Saturday Night Fever*, I could see that Travolta was a talented actor at such a young age. He was about twenty-three.

Lois immediately arranged for me to fly to Los Angeles to meet him. She booked a first-class flight and had a stretch limo waiting for me at the Los Angeles airport to take me to her office. When I arrived, there were about ten women at their desks. I announced myself to the receptionist, "Bobby Ochs here to see Lois."

There was an immediate buzz amongst the women at their desks. Although they were whispering to each other, I heard them saying, "The Bronx Bastard is here." It seems the title that Lois gave me all those years ago she still used. In fact, the working title for this project was *The Bronx Bastard*.

Later that evening, at a Moroccan restaurant, I was introduced to the one and only John Travolta. Some of Lois's staff joined us over dinner. I tried to explain and describe to Travolta, who never gambled, the rush and excitement a young gambler gets when pushing the envelope and going over the edge and betting over your head.

Travolta wasn't getting it, that emotional feeling when you bet over your head or bet your last dollar. I suggested we fly to Vegas for the weekend, and we did the next day, and joining us were Lois, Travolta's high school buddy Jerry Worm, and their two lady friends. We checked in to the MGM Grand Hotel. The plan was to have dinner in the suite Travolta was sharing with his gang, then we would go down to the casino and hit the crap table so he could experience the buzz and high of gambling.

At dinner, he kept asking me to tell stories of my growing up in the Bronx. His interest and that of everyone at the table made me feel good. However, it was work. It felt as if I was doing a one-man show. After Travolta had two of every dessert on the menu, I suggested we head down to the casino. He had another idea. He wanted to go to the show first, where an orangutan trainer had a great act he wanted to see. One of the orangutans, he told us, starred with Clint Eastwood in the movie *Every Which Way but Loose*, so off we went to see a bunch of orangutans.

When it was over, Travolta wanted to go back to the suite for drinks and invite the orangutan trainer. Here I was in Vegas for almost an entire day, had dinner, sat through a show with monkeys jumping around, and was about to have drinks with an orangutan trainer. Not once did we get near a crap table. Travolta was peppering the trainer with all sorts of questions. It turns out this trainer was the third generation of a family that trained elephants to perform a circus act that toured all over Europe. I think he was from Albania.

He went on to tell us he didn't want to train elephants. He wanted to train orangutans. He was disowned by his family and was thrown out of the circus and had to fend for himself. He left, bought a baby orangutan, and for one year spent ten hours a day every day training the orangutan to sit still on a chair for five minutes at a time. *This guy's insane*, I thought and asked if he was for real. His response:

113

"Do you know what you have when you can train an orangutan to sit on a chair for five minutes? You have an act." Well, he certainly had an act with six monkeys jumping around on stage and getting paid for it.

By this time, I was having trouble sitting for another five minutes and said to Travolta, "Let's shoot crap."

Lois was concerned that Travolta, because of his celebrity, would cause a riot in the casino. She called for security but was told that the hotel didn't supply security in the casino and that we were on our own. Now I had to convince Lois that there was nothing to worry about and told her that, when people are gambling and losing money, they're not very interested in movie actors and that once when I was shooting crap in the casino at Circus Circus, where trapeze artists fly over the tables, a trapeze man fell. Everybody in the casino stopped, looked, and went right back to shooting crap. It didn't happen, but I had to get Travolta to the casino. It worked. We laughed and were off to the casino.

Before going with Travolta to the casino, I asked him, "How much are you willing to lose?"

He thought for a moment and said three hundred dollars. While three hundred dollars would be a significant amount to lose in a casino for some of us, not so with Travolta. However, the idea of this trip to Vegas was to see if Travolta could understand and feel what it felt like to put everything on the line. Travolta had just made something like five million on his last picture, so three hundred dollars would not do it. Heck we spent over three hundred dollars on dinner. Travolta had two of every dessert on the menu. I realized my idea wasn't going to work. Nevertheless, we went down to the casino and went over to a crap table.

There was a buzz in the casino when Travolta and I entered. It quieted down. Nobody bothered us, and we exchanged John's three hundred dollars for three hundred dollars in chips. Travolta said he knew nothing about craps. I told him to put a twenty-five-dollar chip on the pass line and explained the intricacies of the game: pass line, don't pass line, the come bet, the place bet, the odds, and so on.

I realized I was bombarding him with too much information. It was short-circuiting his brain, and he was phasing out. I was losing him.

Within a minute, he was down one hundred dollars and not at all enjoying the experience. I pulled him away from the table and said, "Let's forget crap. Have you ever played blackjack?"

He nodded yes.

"Good. Take your two hundred dollars and play blackjack and do whatever you want. You're on your own. Forget about me showing you how to play. Just have some fun."

We stayed in the casino for a little while. Travolta lost his three hundred dollars. It was a long day and night. I was tired and just wanted to go to my room and get some sleep.

The next morning, I ordered breakfast from room service. I just wanted to decompress, be alone with some French toast and coffee. It was Sunday, and the plan was to fly back to Los Angeles later that day, so I figured that after breakfast, I would bet some football games and do basically nothing but watch the games before leaving.

While I was having my second cup of coffee, there was a knock on my door. It was Travolta. He was very animated as he talked to me. I realized he was mimicking me. He thanked me for sharing my stories with him and told me that if *The Bronx Bastard* is ever developed, he would like to play my character. We chatted for a while, and finally, I said, "I want to go down to bet some football games and then try to relax and watch the games in my room."

He got the message and left. I made several trips to Los Angeles and worked with Lois to develop a story line. The project lost traction, and nothing came of it. *What's next?*

Hollywood's Off the Table

With the realization that I was not going to make my fame and fortune in Hollywood, my focus was strictly Samantha and Marigold. Both were doing well, except for the friction between me and Shelly. Joey tried to mediate to no avail. So my attention was Samantha, and I made weekly trips to Marigold to pick up my share, have lunch, and chat with the staff and customers.

Time to move on. Where do I go from here? Hollywood's off the table. My big successes were in hospitality, the restaurant business. Samantha and Marigold were winners, and opening and operating restaurants were my passion. It was what I did and did well. It was time to create a third. *What's next?*

Courting Tennis

Carolyn and I were members at the East River Tennis Club. Butch Seewagen, who was rated the number one tennis pro in New York, was a popular figure around town. He coached the tennis team at Columbia University, was well-known and well-connected in the world of tennis.

One night, while dining with Butch, I told him that I was in the early stages of opening another restaurant in a good location and was in the process of negotiating the deal. I asked him if he would be interested in getting involved. Without missing a beat, he said, "Absolutely! I'd love to."

I laid out the plan for Butch. It was a relatively newly built restaurant on First Avenue and Fifty-Third Street that had recently closed. The owners were never in the restaurant business. It had seating for over one hundred and an outdoor garden with additional seating. The bar sat over twenty. Very little has to be done to get it open. It was perfect. I told Butch the start-up cost would be around two hundred thousand dollars and explained how it would be structured and financed.

Now, the pitch to Butch. I was well-known in the restaurant business and had a good reputation. However, we needed a worldwide name to ensure success. "You know every tennis player," I said to Butch and asked how he would feel if we brought Ilie Năstase, the number one tennis player in the world, into the deal.

Năstase was a colorful character on and off the court. And he was a good-looking Romanian with long flowing hair and known for arguing with the umpire over line calls. So he came naturally to his nickname "Nasty" and was the envy of men for his athletic prowess and adored by women because he was sexy.

"Butch," I said, "Nasty would be the perfect front man. Can you imagine a restaurant on First Avenue called Nasty's? Can you imagine a place with the likes of Ilie and you, where major tennis stars come to eat and drink? With me running the restaurant and the press, everyone in New York will be fighting to get in."

Butch's eyes were getting wider and wider. He was so excited that he spilt his beer on himself. "I'm calling Ilie tomorrow morning," he said, wiping the beer from his lap.

A few days later Butch, Ilie, and I had lunch at Marigold's. I discussed the business plan with Ilie. He loved it. I told him that in addition to lending his name and showing up regularly, he would invest twenty-five thousand dollars. While it was a token amount and disproportionate to the shares he would be receiving, I wanted him to have skin in the game. He agreed.

For the next few weeks while I was negotiating the purchase and working on a new lease, Ilie, Butch, Carolyn, and I were going out almost every night to different restaurants and bars. Everywhere we went, men and women flocked to Ilie. He was an absolute charmer. When I got everything in order, we were ready to close on the deal. We scheduled to meet at Stanley Klein's office on a weekday afternoon. Klein, my attorney, had prepared the documents with the terms of the agreement Butch, Ilie, and I came to. We just had to sign and get Ilie's twenty-five-thousand-dollar check.

Butch and I had our checks with us. A half hour went by, no Ilie. Stanley, Butch, and I made small talk but realized that even though Ilie was always being late, this was too long. I told Butch to call Ilie. He got Ilie at home. He said he wanted to delay signing today and that Butch and I should come over to his apartment to talk there and not in the attorney's office.

On the cab ride over to Ilie's Seventy-Second Street apartment, I was getting more and more steamed. "This is bullshit," I told Butch, "and unprofessional to cancel a business meeting, leaving us waiting and not calling us. We had to call him. I don't get it. Who the fuck does he think he is?" Butch was trying to calm me down, telling me to relax and hear what Ilie has to say.

When we got to his apartment, there was a guy with him. Ilie introduced him as his business manager. Butch and I looked at each other. Ilie never said he had a manager or anyone he wanted us to deal with. All the drinks and dinners over the past month, not a word about a manager. The four of us sat down in Ilie's living room. Ilie, who was always outgoing and charming, was sitting there with his head down, looking at the floor.

This guy started talking. He says Ilie wants to make the deal but is not putting up any money. "Ilie gets paid for endorsing products and wants to get paid for endorsing the restaurant."

I looked at Ilie and said, "That's not our deal."

Suddenly Ilie forgot how to speak. He shrugged his shoulders and put up his palms.

"That's your answer?" I asked. "Let me tell you something, Ilie. Yes, your name is well-known, and if you lend your name to a restaurant that I'm operating, you have to count on me to make sure everything is run first-rate. If not, your name is worth shit. I'm out of here."

The twenty-five thousand dollars wasn't the issue, but letting this guy, whoever he was, try to turn the deal around with Ilie and Ilie squirming and saying nothing was too much. No deal. In retrospect, if Ilie had shown up at my attorney's office and explained that he had second thoughts on the structure of the deal, we would have worked something out. That didn't happen.

Many years later, when I owned Mulholland Drive Café, a restaurant near Turnberry Country Club in Aventura, Florida, I ran into Ilie and invited him to have dinner with me at my restaurant. We both agreed that we each handled that situation badly. I think we missed a great opportunity. *What's next?*

Centre Court, No Nasty

Butch and I regrouped and decided to open a restaurant without Ilie but changed direction and location. My old pal Arnie Rosen and Bob Farley had just secured the lease on a space in a new building directly across the street from Lincoln Center. It was a great location but needed a complete build-out.

On hearing of my deal with Nasty going south, Arnie suggested that Butch and I join him and Farley in building and opening their restaurant on Columbus Avenue on Sixty-Second Street, where the corner met Broadway opposite Lincoln Center. To me, it was a winner. The deal we made was that each of us would have a twenty-five-percent interest and investing equally to the start-up cash.

Prior to this restaurant, Arnie was successful with Farnies, a steak house he owned on Eighteenth Street and Second Avenue. He sold it and opened another steak house with Farley called Meat Brokers on York Avenue and Sixty-Second Street, which they sold just before the Lincoln Center project. The new restaurant would also be a steak house with a standard steak house menu and salad bar.

The marketing plan included running comparison ads in the New York Times showing well-known steak houses such as Peter Luger and the Palm on a chart. Their prices were compared to ours and showed that you got greater value and saved money eating the same quality steak at our restaurant. We named the restaurant Centre Court, which was a nod to Butch Seewagen and his connection to tennis and to the Lincoln Center location. It was a hit. We got off to a great start. Always busy.

At first, Centre Court occupied the street-level space that sat over one hundred and a bar that sat twenty. With the restaurant doing well, we quickly signed a lease for the second-floor space just above Centre Court. We built the restaurant with a kitchen, which doubled our capacity and doubled our expenses—a classic mistake. Doubling the size of the restaurant didn't increase the sales enough to justify the increase in operating expenses and the cost of building a second restaurant. Nothing can break up a partnership quicker than a business running in the red.

We had disagreements, and arguments went on through many angry nights. Finally, Arnie and I agreed to have Farley and Seewagen buy us out. Farley was so determined to split from me and Arnie that he agreed to buy our shares for an amount considerably more than we invested. Arnie and I walked away from a failing restaurant that was losing money every week and made a huge profit.

Farley was the perfect example of making a business decision on emotion. You can't let emotions get in the way. Besides overpaying for our shares, Centre Court had to close with Farley and Seewagen losing even more money. With that experience behind me and Samantha and Marigold doing well, it was time to move on to the next restaurant venture. *What's next?*

Bobby Ochs, Arnie Rosen, Bob Farley, News
Anchor for Channel 11, Butch Seewagen

Butch Seewagen, Morgan Fairchild, Cathryn Fairchild,
Bobby Ochs in front of Centre Court

A Twenty-Twenty Vision

It was 1984 when Carolyn and I met Nick Ashford and Valerie Simpson, the husband-wife duo professionally known as Ashford & Simpson. They wrote and recorded such hit songs as "Ain't No Mountain High Enough," "Reach Out and Touch (Somebody's Hand)," "Solid," to name just a few. My nine-year-old daughter Samantha and Nick and Valerie's nine-year-old daughter Nicole were in the same class at Montessori School. They were classmates and BFFs, so it was easy for me and Carolyn to become fast friends with Nick and Valerie, and we began socializing regularly.

With my background in the restaurant business and Ashford & Simpson's high profile as entertainers, it was natural for us to collaborate on opening a restaurant and nightclub, and we all agreed that the time was right to develop a club that would attract both white and Black clientele, something you didn't see at the time.

So off I went to locate a space in Manhattan for our ambitious undertaking. I wanted something large and dramatic, a big space to make this major statement. The Flatiron District was known for having the size space I had in mind and was just starting to show signs of development. Every day, I contacted real estate brokers and checked the real estate section of the *Times* to find a location.

After a month of looking and not coming close to finding what I wanted, I saw an ad for a space that seemed to be spot-on and called the real estate agent. We met on Fifth Avenue and Seventeenth Street. She took me to a closed restaurant on Seventeenth Street just off Fifth Avenue. Once inside, I could tell that this was not the same space that was advertised and told the broker not to waste my time with phony leads or I was done. She walked me over to Twentieth Street between Fifth and Sixth Avenue to 20 West Twentieth Street. The superintendent let us into this huge space. What first hit me was the thirty or more classic cars parked in the space. Cars from the 1940s and 1950s were all in mint condition. I was more drawn to the cars before looking at the space.

After checking out the classic cars, I looked around the space. It was perfect. It went from Twentieth Street to Nineteenth Street. Fifty-foot frontage, eighteen-foot ceilings, over six thousand square feet. "This is it. I want it," I tell the real estate agent. "And I want to meet the building owner."

She was stunned. "What do you mean?" she almost gasped. I guess she never *sold* a space so quickly.

"I want to make a deal. Let's go to the landlord now."

The owner of the building and the cars was Michael Dezer. We met him that afternoon at Dezer's office on Fifth Avenue and Seventeenth Street. He was about my age, came from Israel with no money to speak of, and built a real estate empire. Our meeting lasted over an hour with me explaining my plan for the space. He offered a lease with very unrealistic terms. I said, "Thanks but no thanks. Goodbye," and left, thinking that it was too bad to lose out on a great space, but I'd keep looking.

Turns out I didn't get the chance. That night, Dezer called me at home. He liked my vision for the space and thought we could make a deal. He said to meet him the next morning and gave me a West End Avenue address.

When I got there the next morning, I was greeted by a beautiful young woman. I was surprised. Dezer told me he lived in a house in Englewood Cliffs, New Jersey, with his family. Hmm. For sure I got the address right. The woman, scantily clad, said, "Hi, Bobby. I'm Nini. Michael is waiting for you on the terrace."

I walked into a beautifully furnished apartment. Dezer was lying on a chaise lounge on an enormous balcony overlooking the Hudson River. After coffee, Danish, and small talk, Dezer and I spent the entire day hammering out an agreement. Not long after, with lawyers and all, the deal was made and the lease signed. Next, I needed an architect to work with to design the massive raw space, and I started interviewing just about every well-known restaurant architect in the city. They showed up with portfolios of their work. All were impressive, but I knew what I wanted and just didn't feel right about any of them.

Ain't No Budget High Enough, Meet David Rockwell

As I was going through the process of finding the right architect for the large project, I got a call from Ed Hershfeld. Ed was the contractor we used to build Centre Court. Ed said, "Bobby, I know you're looking for an architect for your next restaurant. You can do me a favor. I know two young guys who graduated Syracuse University a couple of years ago as architects. They are just starting out and haven't done anything noteworthy at this point. They asked me to call you to set up an appointment. If you could just meet with them, you would be doing me a favor."

I said, "Sure, but I'm not guaranteeing anything. What's their names?"

"Jay Haverson and David Rockwell," he replies.

The next day David Rockwell called. I asked him to meet me on Tuesday at noon in front of 20 West Twentieth Street, the site of the restaurant. At the appointed day and time, as I was approaching the building, there was a young man in jeans. His shirt was half hanging out and half in his pants. He was leaning against the front door. One of his sneakers was untied. I figured he was a delivery boy and said, "Excuse me, you're blocking the door, and I'd like to go in."

He looked at me and said, "Mr. Ochs, I'm David Rockwell from Haverson and Rockwell Architects."

I looked at him and said, "You're shitting me, right? Are you sure you're not cutting geometry class in school?" I must say that I interviewed at least a dozen architects prior to this meeting. They all looked like they stepped out of GQ. So this Rockwell guy got my attention. But after spending the rest of the day sharing my thoughts about this project and having several meetings with him and his partner Jay Haverson, I decided to give them the job of designing this 1.5-million-dollar build-out.

It was quite a gamble hiring this unknown team, but I felt this connection, and they seemed to understand what I wanted to create, a gut feeling that gamblers sometimes get. With my experience and expertise in running restaurants and how things should flow logistically, I was able to understand where the kitchen should be situated and the same with the bar, the restroom, the coat check. Within six months with Rockwall and Haverson's design know-how, we built a multilevel restaurant seating three hundred and a bar holding fifty. Quite an accomplishment.

Nick, Valerie, and I agreed that I would handle all aspects of the build-out, but they wanted to be part of choosing the interior color design. I'll never forget one day sitting with Nick, Valerie, and my wife Carolyn as a painter painted one wall with different color samples. It went on endlessly—one shade of this, maybe a lighter shade, maybe a darker shade—all day long to the point where I was ready to agree to anything. On and on it went into the night. We started drinking with a poke or two on some nice weed. It was getting late. We were nice and mellow to say the least and very hungry. We hadn't eaten all day. I was starving and suggested we stop and get something to eat. No sooner were the words out of my mouth than Nick said, "There's a party uptown. Let's go there—sure to be food." We jumped into Nick and Valerie's chauffeured Rolls-Royce and headed uptown to a town house in the West 90s.

When we got there, all the food was gone. I needed food. Nick said not to worry as he walked over to a woman wearing an apron and asked if there would be any problem getting us some food. "Not at all," she graciously smiled and let me and Nick into the kitchen and told us to sit down at a table. Like two little boys, we watched her fry up fish and side dishes. We devoured every morsel on our plate. Drinking, laughing, and content, we returned to the main room, where Carolyn and Valerie were having a good time with the other guests.

After a while, I was ready to go home, so were Carolyn, Valerie, and Nick. As we were leaving, I said to Nick, "Don't you think we should tip the maid?"

He says, "What maid?"

"The woman who cooked for us," I replied.

He started laughing, saying, "That was no maid. That was Roberta Flack. It's her house."

I was in shock. Roberta Flack just cooked me dinner. I wish I'd known. I would have told her that her song "Killing Me Softly with His Song" was Carolyn and my favorite song when we first met. I did get to tell her when she performed at Twenty Twenty.

Finally, we picked the colors. The menu I created was based on dishes from different regions of the United States: north, south, east, and west. We hired and trained staff. We named the restaurant Twenty Twenty not so much because the address was 20 West Twentieth Street but because we wanted a vision—a club, a restaurant where Blacks and whites could come to dine, drink, and socialize together. But it was 1985, and we were naive and optimistic. Fifty years later, it would have been a success. Unfortunately, at that time, even after a well-publicized and successful opening with every celebrity coming in—Stevie Wonder, Diana Ross, Bill Cosby, Sylvester Stallone, Whitney Houston, Roberta Flack, to name a few—Twenty Twenty closed.

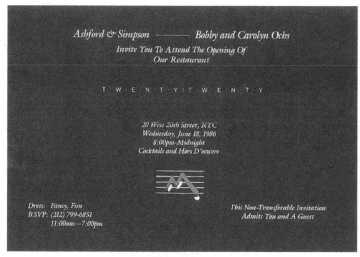

Invitation to the opening of Twenty Twenty

Twenty Twenty Article: Is this the Hottest Spot in N.Y.?

My wife, Carolyn and Ashford & Simpson

Nicole Ashford and Samantha Ochs, age 10

Nicole Ashford and Samantha Ochs, now

Bobby Ochs, Carolyn Ochs, Valarie Simpson and Nick Ashford

The bar at Twenty Twenty

The façade of Twenty Twenty

Speaking of Bill Cosby

B ill Cosby had dined at Twenty Twenty. On one occasion, he booked the balcony space for his annual I Love My Wife Party. Cosby and I worked on the details of the party. He told me that he would supply his personal favorite red wine, and he did. At the party's end, three bottles were left. I asked Cosby if he wanted to take them home. He said, "Hold on to them for when I come back for dinner."

I locked the three bottles in the liquor room. Although I wasn't familiar with the wine, I remembered the name.

A few weeks later, Cosby called and made a dinner reservation and said to have the wine ready when he got there. When I went to the liquor room on the day of the reservation, the wine was gone. In a panic I gave Deena one of my employees the name of the wine and three hundred dollars to replace it, telling her, "Don't come back without it. And if it's more than three hundred dollars, call me and I'll get you the difference." I wasn't about to tell Bill Cosby, America's dad with the number 1 TV show in the country, that his wine had gone missing.

An hour later, Deena returned with the three bottles of Bill Cosby's favorite red wine. She laughed as she handed them to me with 280-dollar change from the three hundred dollars I had given her. Turns out Bill Cosby's favorite wine was six dollars a bottle.

The Black clientele did not want to share what they thought was exclusively a Black club. Whites were uncomfortable and stopped coming. Within a year from opening, Nick and Valerie bought me out, and they closed Twenty Twenty a year later. My other restaurants, Samantha and Marigold, were doing well, and I had an ownership interest in the building that housed Samantha restaurant. We tried to buy the buildings surrounding Samantha to develop a high-rise apartment building but realized soon enough that was not going to happen. We sold the building for 1,450,000 dollars. Not bad since our initial investment was 560,000 dollars and our cash outlay was fifty-six thousand dollars two years earlier.

An Only in New York...

While all of this was going on, I moved my family across the street from our one-bedroom to a large two-bedroom co-op apartment on Seventy-Eighth Street and Third Avenue. It was a rental building that had been converted to co-op. We purchased for 110,000 dollars, and the managing agent asked me if I wanted to put my name on "the list." "What list are you talking about?" I asked.

He said there was a garage in the twenty-story one-hundred-apartment building with sixteen spaces. So sixteen spaces were not enough to accommodate everyone. The list was for co-op owners living in the building. Not owning a car at the time and looking at the long waiting list, what the heck, and I added my name on the long list. It just shows what living in New York can be like.

Ten years went by, and I was in the office in one of my restaurants when I got a call from the co-op board president congratulating me. "For what?" I asked.

He laughed and said, "Your name is next on the list for a garage space." I had completely forgotten about the list. "What kind of a car do you own?"

I told him I'd let him know tomorrow. Not owning a car at the time, the next day, I went out and bought a brand-new Lexus 450 to park in my new space. So with all due respect to Cindy Adams, "Only in New York, kids. Only in New York." Another *what's next*?

A French Connection, Mulholland Drive Café, Patrick Swayze

B ack to restaurants. After selling my interest in the Samantha building and Twenty Twenty, it was time to move on to the next project. It was 1988, and once again, I got a call from Ed Hershfeld, the contractor who connected me with Jay Haverson and David Rockwell. Ed told me a restaurant located on Third Avenue between Sixty-Third and Sixty-Fourth Street was for sale. The owner was a young guy from France who just spent over two million dollars of his father's money trying to recreate Le Cour Saint Germain, a well-known French restaurant in Paris. Within a year, the New York restaurant was doing so poorly that he wanted out.

The young Parisian Claude Tuil, and I met. He showed me around the restaurant. There was no question that he spent at least two million dollars in the place. Everything was top-of-the-line, first-rate. The four-thousand-square-foot space, forty-foot frontage, one hundred foot deep, was fully equipped with a basement that housed walk-in refrigerators, a prep area, and offices. It was very, very tempting to me. Claude had never been in the restaurant business. His father owned a very successful shoe manufacturing company in Paris, and Claude grew up privileged. His father was a tough old-timer who fought as an underground French resistance soldier during World War II and was not happy that his son sunk two million in the restaurant and was losing money week after week.

After a short period of time negotiating with Claude, we agreed to the terms of a buyout. I would purchase the restaurant outright for five hundred thousand dollars. I'd pay 150,000 dollars on closing and 350,000 dollars over four years. The deal was predicated on two conditions. First, I would negotiate a new lease with terms more reasonable than Claude's lease. Second, I would meet with Claude's father for approval of the deal and of me.

The lease part went rather smoothly. I met with the landlord, Joanna Battaglia, and worked out a more favorable lease and got the rent reduced from twenty-four thousand dollars to twenty-one thousand dollars a month plus an extension of five years on the lease and a six-month concession of rent. However, in order to receive these new lease terms, I had to put up six months' rent security, which came to 126,000 dollars upon signing the lease.

Next came the hard part: meeting Claude's father. He was to fly on the Concorde from Paris to New York, stay one night at the Hotel Plaza Athénée on Sixty-Fourth Street and fly back to Paris the next day. No nonsense, no shows, no fancy restaurants—we would meet, and he would decide if he wanted to make the deal.

The day Mr. Tuil arrived, I met with Claude before we headed over to the hotel. Claude told me his father didn't speak English, so Claude would interpret. No problem. Claude and I entered the cocktail lounge off the hotel lobby. There was Mr. Tuil, sitting at a table with a beer. He was a big man in his late '60s, maybe early '70s. His face was wrinkled, not so much from age but from a tough life that saw war and fighting for his country against Nazis during WWII. This was not going to be an easy meeting.

Mr. Tuil clearly was upset that his son lost over two million dollars and that he had to fly to New York to meet some restaurateur who wanted to buy his two-million-dollar restaurant for five hundred thousand dollars and get only 150,000 dollars on signing of the deal and the rest paid over four years.

Claude introduced me to his father. He shook my hand—no smile, no niceties. Claude proceeded to read the terms of the deal in French to his father. After that, Claude turned to me and said his father wants to know what collateral I was offering on the 350,000 dollars. I said, "Tell your father I'm not signing personally, and the collateral he gets if I don't pay is the restaurant back."

Claude looked at me and said he can't tell him that. With that Claude says something in French to his father and then, "No problem. We have a deal," making me the new owner of a French restaurant on the Upper East Side. I would close the restaurant immediately and make it my own.

Next, I called Lois Zetter, who was still managing top Hollywood talent with Bob LeMond, including Patrick Swayze, who was starring in *Dirty Dancing*, which had just been released. I pitched Lois an idea I had for the restaurant. Using her clout and connections, I wanted to have the seven young actors who appeared in the movie *The Outsiders* to get involved in my new restaurant. *The Outsiders* was released five years earlier in 1983, and the actors at the time were relatively unknown. However, because *The Outsiders* was directed by Francis Ford Coppola, it received tremendous recognition. The actors I was talking about were Patrick Swayze, Rob Lowe, Charlie Sheen, Ralph Macchio, C. Thomas Howell, Matt Dillon, and Emilio Estevez. I wanted to get the seven *outsiders* involved in a restaurant called The Outsiders. Publicity would be tremendous.

Lois was on board and said she would fly to New York with Patrick Swayze in the next few days to publicize the opening of *Dirty Dancing* and wanted me to meet him and run the idea by him. The three of us met a few days later at the restaurant in the Park Lane Hotel. She introduced me to Patrick. My first impression of him was contrary to his Hollywood image. He was not the tough, good-looking leading man but someone who was reserved and shy.

As he sat having a bowl of soup and a glass of milk, I ran my *outsider* restaurant idea by him. When I finished, he turned to Lois and asked what she thought. "I love and trust Bobby and love the idea," she said.

Patrick turned to me and said, "I'm in."

With Patrick Swayze on board, I went to work trying to secure the other six actors. Lois and I each spoke to them individually or their managers. None wanted in. When I told Patrick that I couldn't get his costars to sign on and couldn't get the rights to use the name The Outsiders, I'd have to go back to the drawing board. "I'm still in, whatever you do." We shook hands and he said, "I look at you as my big brother." That meant the world to me.

I offered Patrick and Lois each a two-and-a-half-percent interest in the restaurant with no capital investment on their part, just the right to use Patrick's name to publicize the restaurant. They agreed.

With that phase of the project complete, I wanted Jay Haverson and David Rockwell to be the architects. They did a great job at Twenty Twenty and now had three restaurants in their portfolio— thanks to me—and they offered to design my new restaurant with no fee as a thank you for getting them started, an offer I didn't refuse.

Of course, designing a restaurant owned by Bobby Ochs and Patrick Swayze would be a coup and asset to their portfolio. Haverson Rockwell had what I thought was the ideal partnership. Haverson was the more conservative of the two. He was married with a house in Connecticut—very down to earth, a stabilizing influence. Rockwell was more outgoing, more the visionary, more artistically talented, and very personable, which enabled him to attract new clients. Anyway, this job would be less demanding than the complete build-out of Twenty Twenty. This new restaurant project was a facelift and needed a new design. At the same time that I was bringing in the architects, I was looking for investors.

Carolyn and I flew out to Los Angeles to visit my childhood friend Barry Sachs and his wife Helene. Barry and I grew up together in the Bronx and remain close friends. Barry invested with me in Twenty Twenty and was thrilled to be a part of my new restaurant. Barry and Helene had a beautiful house on Mulholland Drive. *Hmm. What a great name for the restaurant: Mulholland Drive Café,* I thought. I called Patrick. He loved it. So now we are building Mulholland Drive Café on Third Avenue on the Upper East Side of Manhattan, then known as the Silk Stocking District.

I set a budget of 150,000 dollars to renovate and open this fully equipped four-thousand-square-foot restaurant. I thought back to Twenty Twenty. Social issues weren't the only problem there. The start-up cost of 1.5 million dollars was way too high. The debt service on the business created its own set of problems. And this time, I wasn't going to overspend. At Twenty Twenty, I didn't put a ceiling on the build-out and opening cost. I let Rockwell and Haverson design a very dramatic, very special restaurant and nightclub. With my approval, we went way over my initial plan of not investing more than a million dollars. This time, I gave explicit instructions to Rockwell and Haverson not to design anything that would go one penny over 150,000 dollars. They agreed.

We decided to meet in a week to go over initial designs. A week later, we met at Rockwell and Haverson's office. They pulled out a full-blown color rendering of the design. Since the name was Mulholland Drive Café, they wanted the well-known scene of Mulholland Drive with couples sitting in 1950s convertibles overlooking the city of Los Angeles aglow with lights to be part of the design. The mural would run the entire one-hundred-foot wall of the restaurant. It would be dramatic, impressive, and a great visual upon entering the restaurant.

However, the design called for several sculptured convertible cars coming out of the wall, a 3D effect with a series of fiber-optic lights blinking over a beautiful painting of Los Angeles. After complimenting them on the innovative design, I asked about the cost. The fiber-optic lighting alone would cost 150,000 dollars. I'd heard enough. "Let me get this straight," I started. "The lighting for the mural would cost 150,000 dollars and that's not counting the sculptured cars, new floors, ceiling, light fixtures, carpentry work, painting, a new front and signage, and what didn't you understand about my 150,000-dollar budget?"

Rockwell kept pushing for the mural until I said, "I'd put photographs of Frank Sinatra and Tony Bennett on the wall like a pizzeria before I went over budget again."

Rockwell stormed out of the room. The more pragmatic Haverson assured me he would talk to Rockwell, and they would make adjustments to accommodate the budget. And they did by designing an eighty-foot mural of Mulholland Drive without the pyrotechnics and going over budget, and it was spectacular.

Rockwell and Haverson went on to designing many other high-profile projects. Eventually, they split. David Rockwell went on to great renown as an award-winning architect and Broadway set designer. His firm employs over six hundred in staff. Several years ago, after Rockwell and I watched a video we made when building Twenty Twenty in 1985, he commented how young we were and asked why I hired him for such a major project. I told him that I recognized his potential and had a gut feeling. He smiled and said he didn't know if he would have hired him.

On the day of Mulholland Drive Café's opening, a huge charter bus pulled up in front of the restaurant. More than sixty women got off the bus and walked into the restaurant. No reservation. One of them told me they were the Patrick Swayze Fan Club from some town in Pennsylvania and just had to be here on its opening. I knew right then that I had something special. We were jam-packed from day one.

During the first week, I was squeezed in next to the host stand when a man came up to me and introduced himself. In a French accent, he told me that he had invested in Claude Tuil's French restaurant and that "I told Claude to do this.'" I asked what he meant by "do this." The man said, "To be busy. To be busy."

I laughed to myself. Sure, open the restaurant door and be busy. Takes lots of hard work to be busy, and that's what it took to make Mulholland Drive Café an instant hit. From the beginning, it was grossing over one hundred thousand dollars a week and did so consistently for years. One hundred thousand dollars a week back in the early '90s was no easy task, especially when menu prices ranged between 9.95 dollars for a half-roasted chicken to eighteen dollars for top-of-the-line sirloin steak. Top shelf liquor was 5.50 dollars a shot for a martini. Today, the same drink would be fourteen dollars. The 170-seat, thirty-five-foot bar was packed every day and night.

I've always believed that "the restaurant business is not about food," and one night, Jackie Mason illustrated the sentiment to a tee. It was the first week Mulholland Drive Café was open. The place was jam-packed and every table taken. The bar was three deep, and there was a one-hour wait for a table. Jackie Mason was having dinner with friends. He calls me over to his table and says, "Bobby, you have a hit here. Do you know why you have a hit? Look at everyone here. They are looking at the people at the bar. Everyone at the bar is looking at the people in the dining room. They are all looking at the mural

141

painted on the wall. They are looking at the floor. They are looking at the ceiling. They are looking at everything but their food. Bobby, you have a hit."

When you have a restaurant that's making money, it's the easiest place to operate. Investors get immediate financial returns. Staff makes money and are thrilled to be a part of a hot restaurant owned by Bobby Ochs and Patrick Swayze. The best help—managers, chef, sous-chef, cooks, servers, runners, bussers, bartenders—all want to work at Mulholland Drive Café and did. As an owner-operator with the publicity of Patrick Swayze being your partner, everybody wants to know you. Everybody wants a table at your restaurant, and just about everybody is offering to invest in your next project.

Along with all of this happening to give me a big head, a night would not go by when women would hit on me as if I was Patrick Swayze. It's amazing what success and celebrity bring out in people. Everybody wants to meet you, dine with you, get a reservation and a good table. We did the wrap parties for several of Patrick Swayze's movies, and he brought the whole cast of *Ghost* to the restaurant.

One night, we set up a long table in the middle of the dining room seated with the likes of Patrick Swayze, Demi Moore, Whoopi Goldberg, and others. I sat next to Demi and her two-year-old daughter Rumer for dinner. Demi was trying to feed Rumer from a bowl of spaghetti when Rumer picked up a handful of spaghetti covered with tomato sauce and dumped it on Demi's head. Rumer jumped off her chair. Demi was in hot pursuit. Quite an off-screen moment for Mulholland diners.

The party for the movie *Road House* had the same long table set up for the cast and crew in the middle of the restaurant. Patrick, Sam Elliot, Kelly Lynch, and Ben Gazzara were there. The day before the party, Patrick gave me tickets to see a private media screening of *Road House*. My general manager Carolyn and I attended. Truth to tell, it was not one of my favorite movies, but the three of us made a pact not to share our views. A small withhold may be considered a lie in some circles but not in mine. Who needs unnecessary, uncomfortable situations?

Some episodes come to mind from the Mulholland Drive Days. One night, while having dinner with Carolyn, I got a call from Patrick. He had just landed in New York and asked if Carolyn and I could wait for him while he had dinner. He arrived, and we spent several hours chatting and enjoying a beverage or two. I usually left before closing, but on this particular night, we left after midnight. Patrick grabbed a cab back to his hotel downtown. Carolyn and I were walking uptown. It was a mild October night. We lived only fifteen blocks away. Any time we walked at night, Carolyn was afraid of being mugged. Whenever someone seemed to be close behind or approaching us, she would tell me, and I would assure her everything was okay. This particular night, everything wasn't okay. I was carrying Carolyn's Louis Vuitton bag on my shoulder. We noticed two young men following us. One of them ran up and got in front of us while the other stood right behind us.

The one in front said, "We could do this the easy way or the hard way. Give me your watch and the bag."

Carolyn panicked, started screaming, and ran out into the middle of Third Avenue, trying to wave down cars. The guy behind us started to chase her into the street, leaving me, wearing my watch and carrying the Vuitton bag with the other guy, who started reaching for the bag. Instinctively, I backed up so my back was against a building. I was reacting and not letting go of the bag and was tussling with this hooded guy in a sweatshirt, who lifted his shirt and pulled a gun from his pants. I can't say what I was thinking, but I was scared out of my mind. I was up against the wall, holding on to a bag I don't give a shit about when the gunman hit me in the face with the butt of the pistol and started to run down the street. His partner was running with him. I took a dive behind a parked car as two shots were fired off. Carolyn made enough noise to stop some cars and frighten the muggers.

As I was kneeling behind the parked car, I looked down at my chest and saw that my light-gray suit was bloody. I thought I was shot, but the blood was a gash from the barrel of the gun hitting my face. If someone had asked me prior to this incident what I would do if I were encountered by muggers on the street, I would say that I would stay calm and give them whatever they wanted. You just don't know how you will react.

I was in a state of shock for some time but went on with business as usual, which was great for my mind and body. We continued to host Patrick's movie parties. At *To Wong Foo, Thanks for Everything! Julie Newmar*, thirty transvestites showed up in full regalia and were having a wonderful time when someone suddenly pulled out a dildo and began passing it around the table. When it got to Patrick, our publicist Bernie Bennett, who was there, jumped across the table and grabbed the dildo from Patrick's hand. He didn't want a picture of Patrick holding a dildo. Although Bernie was trying to protect Patrick, Patrick wanted Bernie fired. It took me two days to convince him that firing Bernie was not happening. Patrick got over it. When you deal with major stars who always get their way, it's not easy convincing them that they weren't getting what they want, but it puts a strain on the relationship.

During my Mulholland years, I had numerous encounters with the garbage carting company and the linen company. They were controlled by organized crime. Sometimes, I negotiated deals with each outfit to reduce what I was contracted to pay. It wasn't easy sitting across the table from these guys. And you couldn't change your carting company or linen company. Every company in the city was controlled by the same mob boss.

Unfortunately, six of these guys met at my restaurant every Monday for dinner. One summer day, when I was in the Hamptons, I got a call from my manager. He told me the FBI was in the restaurant and wanted to wire a few tables to tape the mob bosses. I told him to put the head FBI agent on the phone. I explained to him that the restaurant was a public place and that anybody could come in and dine. And no, they couldn't wire anything. He said he understood and would be back with a warrant permitting the wiring.

Several weeks later, they returned with a warrant and equipment and wired four different tables for the Monday meeting and placed a female FBI agent as a hostess to bring the mob boss to the wired table. And that is how they got to indict these guys. Lesson when dining out: never say anything you don't want anybody to hear when you're in a public place.

In the second year of running Mulholland Drive Café, it was still one of the hottest restaurants in New York. As a result, the Coscan Real Estate Developers out of Toronto and owned by the Bronfman brothers approached me. They wanted me to open and operate a Mulholland Drive Café in the commercial development in North Miami, which is now known as Aventura, and on an inlet off the Intracoastal Waterway. They were building a three-hundred-seat restaurant on the inlet with a dock for boats, a very impressive setting.

We negotiated a deal. I would get possession of a fully built restaurant on the water with a fifteen-year lease. Under the lease terms, there would be no rent until there was a monthly volume of 250,000 dollars, at which point, rent would be calculated in increasing increments, an offer I couldn't but should have refused. It was the early 1990s, and Florida was a two-months-a-year destination from November through New Year's Day.

The only restaurants open in New York on Christmas Day were Chinese restaurants. Upper East Side Jews were known to go to the movies and then to a Chinese restaurant. Knowing this, I decided that I would keep Mulholland Drive open Christmas Day. Actually, I started this practice at Samantha Restaurant, and it was very profitable. So with the popularity of Mulholland Drive Café and the only non-Chinese restaurant open on Christmas, I had a hit.

So Christmas Day, Carolyn and I decided to take in an afternoon movie. We took our place on the very long line outside Cinema 3 on Third Avenue opposite Bloomingdale's. Once entering the packed theater, we found two seats together in the fourth and fifth seats off the aisle in the third row. The three seats off the aisle were occupied by a couple and their coats and packages. Carolyn was not happy that the woman was using the seat for her belongings and insisted she remove them so that we could move one seat over. The woman refused, which led to a screaming match between two Upper East Side ladies, the likes of which didn't usually happen. A movie staffer had to insist that if Carolyn and her worthy opponent didn't stop, they would be asked to leave. Meanwhile, the other woman's husband and I sat there without saying a word. I certainly wasn't getting involved.

Finally, the woman removed her things, but before Carolyn could claim the seat, a single gentleman looking for a seat sat down in the trophy seat. Sitting through the movie *Hoffa*, starring Jack Nicholson and Danny DeVito, was very uncomfortable for all of us. Thank goodness there was someone sitting between the two battling babes.

The movie ended. Carolyn and I left the theater and headed for Mulholland Drive Café for dinner. When we got there, it was packed. No open tables, and there was a half-hour wait for one. While having a drink at the bar, I noticed a couple sitting at a table for four with their coats and packages on the two other seats. Yep, the very same couple from the theater. I pointed them out to Carolyn. She went ballistic and wanted me to throw them out. Normally, it would bother me to see a deuce sitting at a table for four on a busy night. However, I told Carolyn, "Go over to them, introduce yourself, and buy them a drink." She did and won them over. The truth is that Carolyn and this woman were very much alike and had a lot in common as we discovered over the years. They turned into steady customers.

The money I was making over the great run at Mulholland Drive Café afforded me and my family to live a very privileged lifestyle: summers in the Hamptons, trips to Europe, sending Samantha to elite private schools, college at Syracuse University. There wasn't a Broadway show we didn't see. Every restaurant owner invited us to dine. I was daily fodder, mostly good, for Cindy Adams and Page Six in the *New York Post*. When I went to my barber Tony, he would show me a copy of a *New York* magazine article with a picture of me and Patrick Swayze and say almost breathlessly, "Did you see this yet?"

And pro that I was, I said, matter-of-factly, "Yes, I have."

He replied "By the way, who's the guy with you?"

At the time, Lisa Niemi, Patrick's wife, was appearing in the Broadway show *The Will Rogers Follies*. When I went backstage, chorus girls would shout, "Bobby! Bobby!" One in particular jumped on me. It was that way for years. Everything was going great. We were into the eighth year of Mulholland Drive Café and were still one of the hottest and most successful restaurants in the city. I started to notice that the restaurant was showing signs of physical deterioration. When I walked through the kitchen, the floor was buckling beneath me. Years of wear and tear started to erode the kitchen floor in the old building. Hell, it could cave in under the weight of the kitchen equipment and cooks. With that in mind, I looked at the lease and saw that the landlord would be responsible for structural repairs. I set up a meeting with the landlord.

The building that housed the restaurant was a five-story building probably built in the late 1800s. It was next to the Third Avenue El train, making it an undesirable place to live. However, Joanna's father, August Battaglia, had the foresight, or inside information, to purchase this building and several others a year before the Third Avenue El was torn down in 1957. The value of the purchase increased dramatically as the area was developed into the Upper East Side Silk Stocking District and became defined by high rents.

Joanna and I did a walk-through. She saw the kitchen floor. "According to the lease," I said, "the landlord is responsible." She said she would get back to me after speaking to her lawyer.

Several days later, we met again at the restaurant. Joanna informed me that, according to her lawyer, she would replace the wood beam between the kitchen floor and the basement ceiling. That didn't make sense, and who pays for the removal of the kitchen equipment? The removal and replacement of the kitchen floor, the basement ceiling? Any problems relating to this repair?

Joanna turned to me and said without blinking, "That would be your problem." As long as Joanna got a rent check on the first of every month, which, at that time, had been increased to twenty-four thousand dollars a month, she loved my restaurant.

I looked at Joanna and told her that I wasn't paying one dime toward the repair. She replied that all she would do would be the beams, and that's it.

"Well," I said, "we have a bigger problem than the floor. I'm not going to do a thing to the floor, and when one of my cooks falls into the basement and dies, I will be in front of the judge on a liability case. You can bet your last dollar that you will be standing right next to me in front of that judge. Go tell your attorney that."

She was taken aback. Without saying another word, she got up from the table and walked out of the restaurant. Several days went by before she called and suggested that we meet to discuss an offer to make to resolve our differences. We met over a cup of tea the following day. She proposed that I do the repairs and she would extend the lease ten years.

At that time, there were three years remaining on the lease. The restaurant was doing over five million dollars a year and showing no signs of slowing down. The ten-year extension would be of great value whether I chose to operate the restaurant for the extent of the lease or decided to sell. Having an additional ten years was a great asset.

Joanna agreed to keep the existing rent the same for the first five years of the extension and increasing it by only two thousand dollars a month for the final five years. I told Joanna that before we signed the deal, I wanted to bring in a contractor and architect to give me an idea of what the repairs would cost. I met with Denise Hall, an architect, and Larry Lang, a contractor, to give me an estimate. They said it would run 150,000 dollars, and the restaurant would have to be closed for one month while the work was being done. We were heading into summer, so it would be an ideal time to do the repairs. July and August were the slowest months for Manhattan restaurants. It made sense to invest 150,000 dollars, and shutting down for a month was well worth getting a ten-year extension.

We made the deal with Joanna. It all made sense...until the work started. What I didn't consider was that the building was at least a hundred years old and the electrical and plumbing permits, which were grandfathered in, were never upgraded. That was an insurmountable can of worms. The city was all over us, wanting Building Department blueprints to approve the work. With the bureaucracy involved, there was no end in sight. Just the beginning of the end of Mulholland Drive Café.

The original 150,000-dollar estimate blossomed to 650,000 dollars, and the one month anticipated restaurant closing became four months and no income. I literally had to upgrade the building code. Some deal I made. I was going to need additional money. My investors were limited partners and not required to put up additional money. Since I owned the largest share of the restaurant with a sixty percent controlling interest, I felt responsible and did not want to burden my partners.

I devised a plan to secure financing for the project. Metro Media was a company that loaned money to businesses such as restaurants. Their payback was through a barter system. Metro Media would issue credit cards to the public that could be used only at the business that borrowed the money. The holder of the exclusive credit card received a twenty-five-percent discount on charges, and Metro Media retained twenty-five percent toward pay down of the loan, leaving the merchant or restaurant owner with fifty percent. This meant that if I borrowed four hundred thousand dollars, I should be able to pay back the loan in nine months or less. I estimated that out of the 450,000 dollars in monthly sales, forty percent would be from Metro Media cardholders, and it would cost me 260,000 dollars to pay off four hundred thousand dollars over a period of nine months. Based on my calculation, I borrowed four hundred thousand dollars and had to personally guarantee it.

Based on my projections, my plan would have worked. However, what I didn't plan on was that after being closed for four months, business would drop from doing over one hundred thousand dollars a week to eighty thousand dollars a week. I also didn't figure that by this time, almost everyone in New York would have a Metro Media card. And if they didn't have one, once they knew Mulholland Drive Café was on the list, they would get one. Hence, out of the eighty thousand dollars a week in sales, sixty thousand dollars came from Metro Media cardholders. Between the drop in sales and the heavy volume of Metro Media cardholders, I was losing money every week.

I went to Metro Media to explain the situation and told them that if this continues, I will be forced out of business and requested they cap the amount of their share to reduce my loan payment to ten thousand dollars a week, which meant they would receive 2,500 dollars a week to pay off the loan. However, since I personally guaranteed the loan, they refused. I had no choice. I had to go into Chapter 11 to try to save a bad situation.

Eventually I made a deal with chef restaurateur Bobby Flay and his partner Laurence Kretchmer, who owned Mesa Grill, a busy Tex-Mex restaurant in the Flatiron District. They bought me out and opened another Tex-Mex restaurant. In my opinion, I told them, I didn't think that Tex-Mex was the way to go on the Upper East Side. Anyway, the money I got paid off Metro Media and creditors. I got nothing. Unfortunately, I was right about one thing, Bobby Flay's Tex-Mex lasted a year before he closed it down. *What's next?*

L^{We}OVE New York!

...so much, that we've just opened our second restaurant. By Patrick Swayze

Bobby Ochs & Patrick Swayze

Mulholland Drive Cafe

1059 Third Ave., between 62nd & 63rd St., N.Y.C.
Telephone Res: (212) 319-7740
Owners: Patrick Swayze & Bobby Ochs
SOFT JAZZ FROM 9 PM, TUESDAY TO SATURDAY

With its thundering heartbeat and absolutely inescapable energy, Manhattan gives me a feeling I don't get anywhere else in the world. As soon as I leave New York, that feeling leaves, too. When I am away from the city, I miss the constant contact with other people that Manhattan allows – or should I say imposes? You don't get that in L.A. – unless you want to hang out in the Greyhound bus station.

When my wife, Lisa, and I lived in Manhattan from 1972 to 1979, we were struggling to survive as dancers. Those were our formative years, and whenever we return to New York, the city brings back memories of our relationship and our development as artists.

These days I also have the advantage of being part-owner of two of my favorite restaurants in New York, Mulholland Drive Cafe and Bobby O's City Bites. When I'm in New York, Lisa and I dine at one or the other almost every night. My partner at both restaurants, Bobby Ochs, has exhibited a lot of integrity in running both places. He is the reason both succeed. It's exciting that both restaurants are recommended by hotels – that's a real compliment to the food, atmosphere and Bobby.

With their sophisticated palates, the New York dining public is probably on a par with Parisians. We appreciate being accepted by such discerning consumers. I enjoy our customers – they're friendly and classy and the atmosphere lends itself to people saying hello.

560 Third Ave., corner 37th St., N.Y.C.
Telephone Res: (212) 681-0400
Owners: Bobby Ochs & Patrick Swayze

Mulholland Drive Café exterior

Mulholland Drive Café dining room and mural

Mulholland Drive Café façade

Bobby Ochs, Patrick Swayze, Lisa Niemi, and Carolyn Ochs

Barry Sachs, lifelong friend, & Bobby Ochs

Stanley Klein, my friend & lawyer

Bernie Bennett, my longtime publicist

From Patrick to Peaches

It was now the end of the 1990s. Marigold's lease ended. We didn't renew. We had sold the Samantha restaurant building. And without Mulholland Drive Café, I was out of the restaurant business. However, several months before finalizing the Bobby Flay deal, I was offered a closed restaurant space on the corner of Third Avenue and Thirty-Sixth Street. It was half the size of Mulholland Drive Café.

Normally, I would have passed on the deal because it was too small, but I needed to be involved in something before losing Mulholland Drive Café. I was able to immediately raise 350,000 dollars from investors without putting up my own money and built and opened Bobby O's. It was a one-hundred-seat restaurant and bar featuring American comfort food. Patrick Swayze, my loyal friend and partner, invested seventy-five thousand dollars for a five-percent interest, which was seventy-five thousand dollars more than he invested in Mulholland Drive Café. I retained fifty percent with no investment. My reputation as a restaurant operator and the great run at Mulholland Drive Café gave me the leverage to make a deal without a capital investment. *What's next?*

An Offer They Didn't Refuse

During the early days of running Bobby O's and in the final days of Mulholland Drive Café, I got a call from Norman Blank, a friend who lived in Roslyn, Long Island. He explained to me that two of his friends opened a restaurant in Roslyn and needed help. His friends Eli Oxenhorn and Barry Rubenstein had no restaurant experience but owned and opened a restaurant named Johnny Fives. At the time Eli's wife, Sue, wanted to own a restaurant.

After I spoke to Norman, Eli called me and told me that Johnny Fives was open about six months and was losing money every week. He wanted to hire me as a consultant. Mulholland Drive Café and Bobby O's were having their own problems, and the last thing I needed was a restaurant going under.

Reluctantly, I agreed to have dinner with Eli and his wife at Johnny Fives the following Sunday night. Carolyn and I drove to Roslyn. My first reaction as I entered Johnny Fives was that this place is in a state of chaos. Eli greeted us at the door and escorted us to the table where Sue was seated. The four of us sat, waiting for menus and a server—not a good sign when the owner has to wait. People were lined up and standing at the door, waiting for tables. A hostess was nowhere in sight. Phones were ringing, and no one was answering. Tables weren't being bussed. Servers were running around with no visible management on the floor. The problems were glaring.

During dinner, Eli was pitching me to come aboard to fix the problems. The food was lousy. While Eli was pitching, his wife was telling me that window curtains and light fixtures were what was wrong and that when they were upgraded, there would be no problems. She didn't get it. There was no way I was getting involved in this fiasco. Then Eli asked me what I wanted to get involved, I said I'd get back to him.

Driving back to Manhattan, I told Carolyn that Sue was clueless, and I wanted no part of it. Carolyn said that they needed help, and I should do it. How much could I charge to take on this monumental job? As we passed each exit on the Long Island Expressway heading back home, the amount calculated by thousands of dollars. Back home, I said to Carolyn, "I'll make them an offer they must refuse."

Two days later, I met with Eli and Barry at their Madison Avenue office. Sue was there. I explained that Johnny Fives had a terrible reputation. Its image was tarnished beyond repair. They would have to close it and create a new restaurant, a new concept with a new name, and that meant investing more money. And for me to do it, I would need complete control over every aspect of the project—renovating, creating a menu, hiring, marketing, public relations—and I would confer and answer only to Eli. My fee to be project consultant would be twenty-five thousand dollars on signing of the agreement and two thousand dollars a week for as long as Eli and Barry owned the restaurant. To me, this was an offer they had to refuse. Eli and Barry looked at each other, nodded, and Eli said, "Bobby, you have a deal."

The following week, I closed Johnny Fives and started the process of creating a new restaurant. Once again, I was doing what I did best and enjoyed most: another opening, another show. Eli and Barry wanted the new restaurant called *Montgomery* because they grew up in Brooklyn on Montgomery Street. So Montgomery's it was, and after extensive renovation, we opened—all brand-new: chef, servers, bartenders, and a menu similar to the one at Mulholland Drive Café. Bernie Bennett, my forever publicist, did the public relations. It was a hit! Great reviews and word of mouth.

Montgomery's took off from day one. Eli, Barry, and I were happy. The only problem was Sue, who still had no idea how a restaurant was run. I explained to her that any ideas she had had to be discussed with me first. She wouldn't listen. Sue changed policy after policy without telling anyone and drove the chef crazy. After having dinner at a French restaurant and seeing coq au vin on the menu, she would tell the chef that coq au vin had to be added to that night's menu specials. I would then get a call from the chef, complaining about Sue's request and threatening to quit if she didn't stop. I then had to spend an hour with Sue, explaining that we weren't a French restaurant and that the kitchen was not geared for sudden menu changes. But Sue was relentless. If it wasn't the chef whom she was driving crazy, it was the manager or the publicist with some harebrain of an idea.

Generally, I drove to Montgomery's once a week and spent the whole day putting out the fires Sue had started and keeping staff from walking out. Actually, one day, there was a real fire. I was driving on the Long Island Expressway and nearing the Roslyn exit about noon when I saw smoke coming from the direction of the restaurant. The street leading to the restaurant was closed off by police. Montgomery's was in flames. I explained to the police that I ran the restaurant. They told me to leave the car where it was, and I had to walk two blocks to the restaurant, which was engulfed in flames. Firefighters were trying to extinguish the fire.

The restaurant staff and Sue were watching as the restaurant went down in flames. It would be several months before Montgomery could reopen if it could be reopened at all. I spoke to the staff and told them I would let them know what was happening as soon as I knew anything.

I walked over to Sue to commiserate with her as she watched her restaurant going down in flames. Standing next to her was a woman I didn't know. When Sue saw me, she said, "Bobby, I'm glad you're here." Before I could say anything, she introduced me to the woman who was the advertising salesperson for the *PennySaver* newspaper. Sue explained that she promised to place an ad in the *PennySaver* for the restaurant's New Year's Eve party.

I couldn't believe what I was hearing. Her restaurant was up in flames. With all the calm I could muster, I said, "Sue, do you understand that your restaurant is burning down? We don't know the extent of the damage. New Year's Eve is a little over a month away. There is no way that we can rebuild and open by New Year's Eve."

Her response: "But I promised this woman we would advertise with her."

Looking directly at the *PennySaver* ad lady, I said there could be no commitment for a New Year's Eve ad. She nodded and left. With the insurance money from the fire and Eli's adding money, Montgomery was rebuilt and opened in March, ready for another New Year's Eve and an ad in the *PennySaver*.

While the restaurant was closed and under construction, Eli paid the staff each week, which he had no obligation to do. Once Montgomery reopened, I told Eli that I couldn't justify his paying me two thousand dollars a week for basically showing up once a week. We parted ways on good terms. Bernie Bennett, my publicist, wanted to place an article in the newspaper, saying that I was no longer associated with Montgomery Restaurant in Roslyn. I let him do it and regret it to this day. It served no purpose.

While Mulholland Drive Café was still open, we opened Bobby O's. It was summer, and the warm weather allowed me to open the sliding patio doors on Third Avenue for outdoor seating. Public relations for Bobby Ochs and Patrick Swayze's new restaurant made it an immediate go-to place. We were jam-packed from the get-go. It was primarily a young singles crowd. That concerned me.

When the season went from summer to fall and then to winter, the patio door had to be closed, which meant no outdoor seating. It would be a game changer. The restaurant was in a small space. Ceilings were low, and I made the mistake of designing the interior with a metal ceiling and a ceramic tile floor, which made for a very noisy restaurant when full. The combination of a noisy restaurant chased older diners away and fickle young singles crowd found new places to hang out—a disaster!

Recognizing this, I decided to close the restaurant. Now for the first time in over twenty years, I had no restaurant to operate. I sat home, trying to figure out my next move. I missed the action of running a restaurant: being involved in every aspect of it, interacting with staff, schmoozing with guests, being the center of attention. I needed another restaurant the way a junkie needs a fix. And just as much as I needed a restaurant to be part of my life, I needed to create it. I needed it to be mine for better or worse and knew that I needed a celebrity partner. I tried to think of who would be my next celebrity hook, the next star to incorporate into my next project. Marla Maples came to mind. Why Marla Maples? *What's next?*

Peaches Grows on Sixty-Third Street. "Hello, I'm Gay Talese"

M arla Maples and her mother often dined at Mulholland Drive Café. Marla said that she would be interested in opening a restaurant with me. She also told me something I didn't recall. We had met years earlier when I owned Twenty Twenty when she was a young aspiring actress and model and newly arrived in New York from Dalton, Georgia.

With that in mind, I contacted Marla, and we set to meet at the Four Seasons Hotel on East Fifty-Seventh Street for drinks to discuss my thoughts on a project I had in mind. Over drinks, I convinced her to be a part of a new restaurant venture. At the time, she was married to the once and always Donald Trump and going through a messy divorce. She was eager and looking forward to doing something new and apart from him.

With Marla on board, I had to find a location and financing. I had neither. In past restaurant deals, I would first decide on the concept, find the location, negotiate the terms of the lease, and secure the space with my own money. After getting the space, which was usually an empty restaurant or one going out of business. I then would find the star celebrity, and then I would find investors to finance the project. It was a bit of a gamble to secure a restaurant space on my seed money, and I hoped that I could sell the idea to investors.

Even with names like Patrick Swayze and Ashford & Simpson, it's not easy standing in an empty space with potential investors without restaurant background to have them see my vision. However,

I always managed to get the financing. Now it would be different even with Marla Maples's involvement. She was well-known, and I believed she could get the restaurant immediate recognition, especially with her divorce from Trump in the tabloids on a daily basis.

Normally, the next phase would be to secure a space, but I was short on money, and my cash flow was low, so that was out. I needed investors before finding a location. The deal I had to sell investors was that I needed one-hundred-percent capital backing for a fifty percent interest. Marla would receive a ten-percent interest for the use of her name and to be at the restaurant as an occasional host. I would keep forty percent plus a salary for operating the restaurant. With no investment from Marla or me, this was going to be a tough sell even with my good reputation as a restaurateur, which was somewhat tainted after having to sell Mulholland Drive Café and closing Bobby O's. Investors would want me to put up my own money to have skin in the game. So this was not going to be an easy sell.

I began making calls to the list of people who previously invested with me. I got pretty much the same response: "Let me know when you find a location and how much is needed, then we'll talk." A Catch-22 for sure, how could I secure a space with no money and get money without a restaurant space? Nobody was willing to back me and Marla blindly.

Generally, I'm not a believer in fate. I believe you control your own destiny by knowing what you want and then making it happen. I was running out of options and was walking across Fifty-Seventh Street midweek with no destination in mind, just thinking of where to get investors. While deep in thought, I looked up and saw a familiar face, Stuart Alpert. Stu, who was in the real estate business, was one of the investors in Marigold, where we all did well financially. For some reason, and I can't remember why, I hadn't contacted him for the Marla Maples venture.

Stu and I greeted each other and exchanged small talk: "How's the family?" "How's your family?" and so on. He said he was meeting his son at Le Colonial, a popular restaurant on Fifty-Seventh, and asked me to join them.

As we headed to the restaurant, I told him about Marla Maples and the new project and would like to run it by him over lunch. After a two-hour lunch, Stuart invited me to come to his office in Westchester the next day to meet with a group of fifteen investors who invest in start-up deals. He was interested in my deal and wanted me to pitch it.

The next day, I drove to his office. In a conference room with fifteen tough real estate guys and Stuart sitting at a long table, I sold the deal. They would fund my next restaurant with Marla Maples under my terms, and Stuart would represent the group in dealing with me. There was no way that I could or would run a restaurant and deal with fifteen investors. A budget was set at 750,000 dollars to find a location and open a restaurant. Again, while I don't generally believe in divine intervention, if I didn't run into Stuart Alpert on Fifty-Seventh Street and have lunch with him and his son, who knows if I would ever have found the money needed for my next restaurant?

Now came the serious search for a location. I was concentrating on the Upper East Side where I was well-known and had owned successful restaurants. I was told about an Italian restaurant on Sixty-Third Street just around the corner from where Mulholland Drive Café had been located that was up for sale. Bobby Flay's Tex-Mex restaurant was gone, and I thought Sixty-Third Street would be a good location. The only drawback was that it was on a side street. However, with my reputation in the area and Marla's name and presence, it could work.

Marla and Stuart agreed, and I started to negotiate the purchase of the Italian restaurant, which we would close and renovate. The restaurant occupied the basement, street level dining room, and the second floor of a five-story building. I made a deal with the two owners of the restaurant. They were thrilled to unload their failing restaurant. We set a date to meet at their lawyer's office to finalize the deal. *What's next?*

A few days before the closing, I was at home about seven in the morning when the phone rang. I answered, and the voice on the other end asked, "Is this Bobby Ochs?" I said it is. The caller introduced himself, saying, "Hello, I'm Gay Talese. I'm a writer. I'm not sure if you know who I am."

I said yes, that I knew who he was and loved his book *Honor Thy Father*. "What can I do for you?" I asked.

He explained that he was writing a book based on the building at 200 East Sixty-Third Street where my soon-to-be restaurant would be opening. He was intrigued, he said, with the history of all the commercial and restaurant tenants who had occupied the building from the time it was built in the late 1800s or early 1900s and had gone out of business, and he wanted to interview me. "Bobby," he said, "what are you doing now? Would you like to have coffee with me at my town house on Sixty-First and Park to talk about your project?"

I accepted and walked from my apartment on Seventy-Eighth Street to meet with him.

When I rang the bell at Talese's four-story town house, he answered the door and invited me in, and a very dapper Gay Talese escorted me around his impressive home office, where he does his research and writing. He poured us coffee and asked, "Marla Maples? Why do you want Marla Maples as a partner? You're a well-known restaurateur, why Marla Maples? Are you fucking her?"

"What business is that of yours?" I shot back. "And if I were, I wouldn't tell you." Just doing what Gay does, I thought. Always the investigative reporter.

He told me that he wanted to follow me through all phases of opening the restaurant—from the closing with lawyer, to creating the concept, to designing and construction, to hiring staff, creating the menu, publicizing, and opening. Sounded good to me. We planned to meet the morning of the closing to go to the lawyer's office, and I picked him up the next morning in a taxi. I let Stuart know about Gay's book and that he would be at the closing. Stuart was a big fan of Gay's and loved the idea that Gay would be there.

At the closing, I introduced Stu and Gay. When I introduced Gay to the sellers, they said they didn't want Gay there and showed him to the waiting room, where he stayed until the deal was done. The sellers owned other restaurants, but they really weren't restaurant operators, and they had other business interests. Restaurants were not their source of income. Apparently, owning a restaurant was a bad decision for them, and they didn't need any publicity that could or would come from a Gay Talese book.

Throughout the process of building and opening the restaurant, Gay came by periodically. During that time, he changed direction with his book. When he finally finished his book years later, it was titled *A Writer's Life*, and little was written about the building and my restaurant. Gay must have lost interest when he discovered that I was the son of the Adolph Ochs, who made Trotsky's false teeth and not the son of the Adolph Ochs who was the publisher of the *New York Times*. And he never again asked if I was fucking Marla Maples.

During the designing phase of the restaurant, Marla and I and the architect worked closely. At Marla's insistence, I hired an expert in feng shui, the ancient Chinese art of balancing energy forces to enhance and harmonize individuals with their surrounding environment. Marla said that Donald was known to have used a feng shui expert. To me, it was an added expense we could do without, and I didn't need anyone telling me how to enhance the flow of energy in a restaurant. I designed restaurants my entire adult life, but it was important that Marla have input. For the record, it was no easy task convincing Stuart and the fifteen investors that we were hiring a feng shui expert, but we did. They suggested what would make for good energy. Happens they were right, but it didn't help.

Throughout the building of the restaurant, Marla was going through a difficult time with Trump and their divorce. Almost every night, she called me, crying that he was only giving her a million dollars plus child support for their baby Tiffany, which is what their prenuptial agreement called for. According to Marla, if she and Trump divorced before five years, she would get a million dollars and child support. If she signed the agreement, what did she expect? I wanted to know. She responded that Donald promised that if they would get divorced prior to the fifth year of marriage, he would increase the amount to five million. One problem: that wasn't written into the agreement. In the end, Marla couldn't withstand the negative tabloid press she was getting while the restaurant was being built. So she took baby Tiffany and went to Los Angeles. We spoke daily, and I filled her in on the progress of the restaurant.

Finally, we had to give the restaurant a name. We each suggested names. We each rejected names. This went on until I said, "Marla, we have to make a decision. Time is running out." I don't remember whose idea it was, but we finally agreed that *Peaches* sounded good and made sense since Marla was from Georgia, the Peach State.

After agreeing on the name, I asked Marla how it should be spelled. She asked what I meant. "Well, we can spell it P-E-A-C-H-E-S, which means it's plural, more than one peach, or we can spell it P-E-A-C-H-'-S, meaning that the restaurant belongs to a person who is a peach."

Without hesitation, she chose the plural Peaches, and all applications for licenses were under the Peaches name. A Peaches logo was designed for the outside canopy and the menus. Everything was a go. My publicist Bernie Bennett sent out releases to the media that Bobby Ochs and Marla Maples's new restaurant Peaches would be opening soon. I sent Marla a first-class ticket round trip to New York from Los Angeles. The investors were not happy about paying ten thousand dollars for her ticket.

It was a few weeks to the opening, and I was showing Marla around the newly renovated restaurant. The basement kitchen was great. The street level dining room was beautiful. The second-floor bar and lounge, with its private party room, was sensational. She loved it all. "Bobby," she says while we were standing outside under the canopy displaying the Peaches logo, "I'd like to ask you a favor. I want to change *Peaches* to *Peach's*."

"What?" I said in disbelief.

She explained that she might get a part in a new TV show playing a character named Peach, who owned a restaurant called Peach's. My response is unprintable, except for the "no way" part.

After several minutes of Marla's sobbing, she understood that the name had to remain Peaches. By the way, the TV show never panned out either. *What's next?*

"Knucklehead" by Anthony Bourdain, Chef

I was now interviewing chefs to run the Peaches kitchen and execute a menu the chef and I would create. We would have daily specials. One day, I got a call from an employment agency. They said they wanted me to interview a very talented chef who was just out of a rehabilitation program. "Send him over," I said.

The next day the chef arrived and introduced himself. "I'm Anthony Bourdain," he said. Yes, that Anthony Bourdain in 1998. I must have spent two or three days with him, explaining what I was looking for in a chef and listening to his ideas. I'm not sure why I didn't hire him. The chef I hired was then running the kitchen at a well-known restaurant.

Years after meeting Bourdain, he wrote *Kitchen Confidential*. In it, he referred to me as the "knucklehead that was Marla Maples's partner." He wrote that he intentionally dumped the interview for the chef's position. I have no recollection of why I did or didn't hire him or why he said I was a knucklehead. *C'est l'Anthony*. May he rest in peace.

Trump Gets in by One Vote

O pening night at Peaches was by invitation only. It was going to be Marla's night. Every celebrity and VIP was on the guest list, including New York's mayor, Giuliani. Trump was not invited. Marla didn't want him ruining the night.

Opening night was packed. Everyone who was anyone in New York was there. There was tremendous preopening publicity and a crowd of gawkers stood outside the restaurant to see who was arriving. Sure enough, the uninvited Trump arrived. He insisted that he wanted in. Security at the door stopped him. The media was all over outside and inside. Marla was upset. The press would have had a field day with the scene that Trump was creating. I told Marla, "My vote is let's take the high road and let him in." Reluctantly, she agreed.

In walked Trump. The first thing *ET* (*Entertainment Tonight*) did was to get him and Marla together on camera with Trump saying to Marla in a very nasty, tone, "I wish you a lot of luck here. I hope you make a lot of money because you're going to need it."

She started crying and ran into the kitchen to get away from him and the TV cameras. Trump got what he came for and succeeded in ruining Marla's night. Marla was right. He should have been kept out. Bad vote letting Trump get in.

Peaches opened to the public to favorable press reviews the next day. After that, the main floor dining room that sat one hundred was busy most nights, so was the second-floor bar and lounge that featured live music.

Marla's heart was not in it. She couldn't handle New York and Trump and flew back to live in Los Angeles. After that, the restaurant didn't have the right energy even with the kitchen and wait staff producing a first-rate dining experience. Neither Bobby Ochs nor feng shui could keep Peaches going. Despite taking a 750,000-dollar loss, what bothered Stuart and the fifteen investors most was hiring the feng shui expert and paying for Marla's round-trip airfare to and from Los Angeles and New York. They all knew I ran a professional operation, and through no fault of mine, it just was not meant to be. Apparently, Gay Talese was on to something about location, location, location. Too bad he gave up on writing the original book. *What's next?*

RUSH & MOLLOY

BY GEORGE RUSH AND JOANNA MOLLOY

Peaches & creamed by The Donald

Donald Trump turned up Wednesday adding a dollop of publicity to Peaches — the new restaurant his estranged wife, Marla, has cooked up. But the smiles they showed the cameras just barely concealed the bitter aftertaste of their marriage.

More than a year after the Trumps announced their split, they are still in court over whether Marla should get more than their prenuptial agreement allows. According to The Donald's lawyer, Jay Goldberg, a settlement was proposed, "but when things are not accepted, offers are withdrawn. At this point there is no settlement offer even on the table."

So that set the scene for Trump to walk into Peaches and proclaim that he hoped the E. 83rd St. eatery would be "a success for Marla's sake — because she is going to need the money."

Marla, who's said to have a new beau in California, greeted the remark with a smile, but confided a little later: "Can you believe he said that?"

Donald wouldn't get into the divorce with us, but he says he wishes the best for the "very talented" Marla. "I always like to support people, especially my ex-wives."

JUST PEACHY: Tiffany Trump's parents, Donald and Marla, made nice at Wednesday's opening of Peaches, Marla and Bobby Ochs' new restaurant.

Article in Rush & Molloy

EW YORK POST, TUESDAY, MAY 26, 1998

Marla and pal have a peachy keen new idea

Cindy Adams

GUESS who's going into trade?

Miss **Marla Maples Trump** the actress.

Opening a restaurant, she is.

Formerly — like a whole head-lined adultery, marriage, and split ago — she was slugged the Georgia Peach. And so what's this eatery to be named?

Peaches.

Opens mid-August.

Her partner's **Bobby Ochs** who once owned Mulholland Drive Cafe with his then-partner **Patrick Swayze.** It was on Third Avenue at 63rd. And this child from Georgia, the Peach State, where's her new joint to be?

Around the corner. On 63rd be-tween Third and Second.

Marina Garnier
MARLA MAPLES
Food for thought.

Peaches Restaurant

From Peaches Gone Bad to an Inedible Spread

I t was getting to be a pattern, and once again, I was without a restaurant and spent the next year working with Marc Packer to open Rue 57 on Fifty-Seventh Street off Sixth Avenue. Marc Packer is one of the best restaurant operators in the business. He created a string of successful restaurants, including Abe & Louie's, Harley-Davidson Café, Tao, Rue 57.

While working with Marc in opening Rue 57, the Podolsky brothers, who owned several hotels in the city, approached me. They offered me a full partnership to build and operate restaurants and bars in all of their hotels. It was hard to refuse a fifty-percent interest without having to invest my own money. They said they wanted me for my expertise and reputation. I told Marc Packer. He agreed it was an offer I couldn't refuse. With that, I signed a contract and left Rue 57.

After signing the contract with Jay and Stuart Podolsky, we selected the Marseille Hotel on the corner of Twentieth Street and Third Avenue for me to create the first restaurant in their chain of hotels. At the time, there was a diner off the hotel lobby that was closed. My concept for the restaurant was to have a menu of small dishes like minisliders, mini-crab cakes, appetizer-size entrees, and a sushi bar. The concept was that guests could share and experience an assortment of dishes along with exotic cocktails. The large bar we built would attract a drinking crowd. The dining area would be less traditional and more loungy to complement the grazing menu.

171

During construction, we decided to include the basement area in the design and, while clearing out the basement, we discovered three large domed all-brick vaults under the sidewalk. After seeing the vaults cleaned up, I thought they would be perfect as private party rooms for exclusive bottle service. They would also create a chic two-level restaurant bar and downstairs lounge.

Bernie Bennett, my longtime publicist, had recently passed away, so I hired David Granoff, a publicist I met while at Rue 57. We got great publicity and good reviews from the new restaurant in the Marseilles Hotel, which we named Spread. The restaurant was an instant success, jam-packed from day one.

Now I was ready to tackle the Podolskys' next hotel, The Amsterdam on West Forty-Sixth Street, but the Podolsky brothers had other plans. Thrilled with the money generated by Spread, the restaurant I had created, they now had the blueprint for success and wanted to cut me out of my fifty-percent share of profits and refused to honor our contract. They came up with a phony breach and forced me to fight them in court. What followed was a messy lawsuit.

Foolishly, we agreed to have a judge decide the case—no jury. Big mistake on my part. After months of litigation, my attorney and I were sure that the judge would find in my favor. The Podolskys had clearly breached our contract, so we were blindsided when the judge found in favor of the Podolskys. Something didn't smell right.

Some years later, *New York* magazine did an expose on the Podolsky Brothers and characterized them as the most despicable businessmen in the city. That was true. The article accused them of illegal practices, at stopping at no expense or other means to screw business associates and anyone else who would get in their way.

Spread, the restaurant and club, continued to do well for some time after my departure, until one night, there was an altercation at the bar. Someone pulled out a gun and killed a man at the bar. The state liquor authority immediately took away Spread's liquor license and shut the restaurant down. Unfortunately, a man lost his life, but it was fitting that the Podolskys should lose Spread. *What's next?*

Another Opening, Another Show. Enter Britney Spears

Around this time, I heard that the restaurant in the Dylan Hotel had closed and that Morris Moinian, its owner, was looking for a restaurant operator for the closed space. The Dylan was a small boutique hotel located on Forty-First Street between Park and Madison Avenues, which is definitely not a good location for a restaurant.

The restaurant that had closed was a five-star French restaurant. I don't know why it closed. Maybe too pricey, maybe wrong location for high-end French cuisine, maybe poor management. No matter, the large space was empty and available.

Moinian contacted me and asked if I was interested in opening a restaurant in the space off of the hotel's lobby. We met to discuss the possibilities of coventuring a deal. At the meeting, I told Moinian my concerns. First, it was a lousy location. Second, the restaurant space, located in the back of the hotel lobby, had no street presence. While it did have a well-equipped kitchen in the basement, the main dining room and the second-floor balcony needed major renovation, which required a large investment of money.

Moinian asked me if I could bring in a celebrity to be part of the restaurant. "Morris," I said, "I believe the only way to get a restaurant in this location on the map would be to bring some star power for much-needed publicity, and if I bring a celebrity into the deal, you have to finance the project."

He agreed and said, "See what you can do."

BY DAVID HINCKLEY

OF ALL the teen singers who populated the radio and celebrity magazines way back in the early 21st century, Britney Spears was probably the most legitimate candidate to open a restaurant, because whatever her merits or demerits as an artist, at least she looked like she had eaten a meal sometime in the last month.

In a world where most of her rivals were as thin as their singing talent, Britney had no trouble declaring she enjoyed a good plate of fried chicken.

Also, since young Ms. Spears was routinely described in print as a "pop tart," perhaps she felt a cosmic obligation to enter the foodstuffs field.

So she, like, did.

EARLY IN 2002 her people cut a deal with one Bobby Ochs to open an eatery in the Dylan Hotel at 52 E. 41st St. Ochs was a chef who specialized in partnering with celebrities, figuring a famous name would bring patrons in the door once and his cooking would lure them back. This had worked nicely with Patrick Swayze, with whom Ochs had a 10-year partnership in Los Angeles, although less well with Marla Maples, the former Donald Trump wife whose restaurant Peaches lasted less than a year.

Spears would be "fully involved" in the design and execution, Ochs assured everyone. Indeed, Britney, who had just turned 20 and whose income that year was estimated at $38 million, named the place herself: "Pinky," which was the name then-boyfriend Justin Timberlake was apparently fond of whispering in her ear.

When the relationship with Timberlake ended, however, so did Pinky. The joint would now be Nyla, which everyone assumed to be the initials of New York and Spears' native Louisiana. Actually, it was more a lift from Nyla's Burger Basket, a Mississippi fast food joint that Spears frequented on her trips down home. Nyla was the name of the owner, Nyla Price.

Nyla's Burger Basket, where the biggest culinary decision was whether to order the combo with fries, was a little more basic than Britney's Nyla. The New York Nyla featured "home-style" Cajun food, which meant crab cakes for $20, $16 roasted pork chops, a $16 Nyla Burger and various more exotic items such as "Southern sushi" and lobster mashed potatoes.

In contrast to Nyla's Burger Basket, which had itself a "Britney Room," the New York patrons enjoyed no such intimacy with the star. Nyla displayed no Britney memorabilia, which Ochs explained was a deliberate marketing decision.

This was a serious restaurant, he solemnly explained, not some sort of novelty tourist attraction.

DAILY NEWS   June 6, 2005

HOME STYLE
BRITNEY'S RESTAURANT, 2002

I left Moinian thinking, *Okay, now what?* I had a space and financing but no clue how to get a celebrity involved.

When I got home that night, I told Carolyn about my meeting with Moinian. She told me she had been at the dentist that day. Our dentist Jason Karsarky was married to Susan, who had been the catering manager at Mulholland Drive Café. We were all good friends. Carolyn went on to tell me that Jason's next-door neighbor was a theatrical manager, and Britney Spears was his client. That's all I had to hear, and I immediately called the dentist and asked him to set up a meeting with Britney's manager.

It was 2002, and Britney Spears was the hottest performer on the planet. I contacted her manager Larry Rudolph and arranged to meet him at his office the next day. He said he knew and loved all my restaurants and that I was well regarded as a restaurant operator. Just what I had to hear as I was about to pitch my project.

After I laid out the plan, Larry was all in and thought Britney would love the idea. But before I could present anything to Britney, Rudolph told me I had to get approval from Britney's financial manager Bert Podell. Larry set up a meeting for me and Podell.

When I got to Podell's office, he told me he had been to my restaurants and knew that I had a solid reputation. While schmoozing, he mentioned that his hobby was baking. After an hour of going over the plan for Britney's role in the restaurant venture, Bert liked it and said he would discuss it with Britney and her mother, Lynne, and he arranged for me to meet with her.

The day before the meeting, I went to a restaurant supply store and bought a professional KitchenAid commercial baker's mixer and had it delivered to Podell at his office. On the day of the meeting, Podell was there with Britney and her mother. I showed them around the empty restaurant and presented them with my vision and the structure of our deal. Britney would receive a one-third interest for the use of her name in promoting the restaurant. I would receive a one-third interest for building and running the operation. Neither Britney nor I would invest money for our interest. Moinian would be a one-third partner and the moneyman. Within a week, we agreed to terms and signed a contract. As operating partner, I was in full control of all decision-making.

I was back in business with a major celebrity where I belonged. Now began the work: designing, building, creating a menu, hiring and training staff, promoting of Britney Spears's yet-to-be-named restaurant.

The first thing I did was hire Jay Haverson, David Rockwell's ex-partner, to design the restaurant. I knew Jay would be hands-on. Rockwell now had a large architectural firm with junior architects and was working on multiple projects all going on at the same time. Rockwell's contact was with the staff, not the client. In fact, when I was looking for an architect for Peaches, I made an appointment to meet with Rockwell at his office.

Over the years and since Twenty Twenty, we were in touch. I waited almost an hour until someone from his staff showed me to her office. Her assignment, she said, was to talk to me about designing the restaurant. When I asked her when David Rockwell would be joining us, she said, "He's too busy. I am your project manager."

I couldn't believe what I was hearing. Rockwell, whom I gave his first major job, was blowing me off. I said, "No disrespect to you, but I'm out of here."

As I was leaving the building, Rockwell was standing with a group of his staff. I walked over to him and said, "David, are you too busy to say hello?"

He retorted, "Hello," and turned his back to me.

What the fuck, I thought. Fuck him. Success has strange fallout, I guess. Or could be because I didn't hire him when Mulholland Drive Café was renovated. I never found out, but in later years, we have spoken and had pleasant conversations.

Haverson and Rockwell were no longer partners. Haverson now had a small firm, which I preferred for the Britney Spears restaurant. Jay would work hands on with me, and once the plans were complete, Jay, Moinian, and I approved them. Britney left all aspects of the restaurant operation to me. We agreed to the budgeted 1.2 million dollars, which Moinian would finance for the build-out and opening expenses, and he would have a one-third interest in the

Britney Spears restaurant in his Dylan Hotel, which would enhance tourism and increase Dylan Hotel's reservations and related income. And Moinian would be getting twenty-five thousand dollars a month rent.

We agreed to name the restaurant Nyla, a nod to New York and to Louisiana, Britney's home state. The menu would be classic Cajun and standard New York cuisine. In the early stages of construction, there were trouble signs. Haverson and I were acting as construction managers and hired all subcontractors, carpenters, electricians, plumbers. Either he or I knew them or had worked with them on other projects. They were excited and eager to work for us, especially because Britney Spears was involved.

After the second week of construction, we needed twenty thousand dollars to pay various contractors for materials and labor. I told Moinian. He said, "See me tomorrow," which is not what I or the workers wanted to hear, and he could easily write a check on the spot.

"No problem," I say to Moinian.

The next day, he gave me five thousand dollars and told me to spread it around to keep "things going." I took the five thousand dollars and knew that there were going to be major problems with Moinian paying the contractors. It just didn't add up. Morris Moinian was a very, very wealthy man. He grew up privileged in Great Neck, Long Island, one of the wealthier areas in Nassau County. His family left Iran with millions. His brother Joseph Moinian was one of the wealthiest real estate men in New York City with major holdings. Morris owned the Dylan Hotel and was CEO of a major garment center company. He lived in a penthouse on Park Avenue with his wife and three children. Why would he be stiffing workers? Because he could? Because this was how he did business? I didn't know but knew there was going to be a problem going forward.

The contractors went along with being paid piecemeal and continued working under those conditions, knowing that Moinian was a billionaire and because of Britney Spears's name. They also knew that they had never been stiffed by me or Jay. The job was moving along on schedule. The build-out was progressing, but we were falling behind on paying workers each week.

Haverson designed a magnificent glass staircase and walkway that connected the main dining room to the second-floor balcony at a cost of 125,000 dollars. He knew the construction crew at General Motors in Detroit, and they built the elaborate staircase from his drawings. No one from General Motors ever came to the restaurant. It was built in Detroit and transported to New York in two pieces on two giant trucks. I watched in awe as a crew of eight men with a mechanical lift assembled and installed the staircase the first time they tried. Amazingly, it fit perfectly, not one adjustment. What a feat, and what was even more amazing was that General Motors built and installed this masterpiece without asking for or getting a down payment.

When Moinian got the 125,000-dollar bill from General Motors, he promised to mail them a check. Weeks later, he still hadn't sent the check. A week before construction was scheduled for completion, four hundred thousand dollars was still due to contractors, and the 125,000 dollars was still not paid, and the contractors wouldn't finish the job until they got paid, which meant we couldn't open. Moinian claimed he needed time to raise the money—not good and bull. Britney's busy schedule dictated the opening date and could not be delayed. Publicity and invitations were out for the major red-carpet event. We got permission from the city to close down Forty-First Street on opening night. There was too much riding on the job's being finished and opening.

After long and tortuous negotiations, Haverson and I convinced the contractors that they would be paid from revenue generated once Nyla was open for business. I knew that was a recipe for disaster, but they finished the job, and we opened on time.

The day of the opening night party, there were torrential rains that lasted all day and all night. Forty-First Street between Park and Madison Avenues was closed. Bleacher seats with a tent were erected for the press. We hired security for crowd control. Britney was to arrive that night to walk the red carpet. Every major news outlet and TV and print press from around the world were sitting in the bleachers getting soaked. At one point, the tent caved in from the rain. Just what we didn't need.

Eight o'clock came and went—no Britney. Crowds, mostly young girls, were getting soaked while waiting to get a glimpse of Britney. At nine thirty, she showed up with Annette Wolff, her publicist. The schedule was that Britney would be interviewed by the press. Instead, she walked the red carpet, and Wolff would let only one reporter question Britney, who gave a one-sentence answer and was whisked away into the restaurant by Wolff. The press went bonkers and started booing. Nyla was in deep, deep trouble, no doubt about it. It wasn't long before the press wrote negative reviews. This added to the pressure of paying the contractors and problems with Moinian.

Several weeks before the date set to open, I was at a meeting with my management team of four front-of-the-house managers, the chef, and the sous-chef. Much had to be accomplished in a short time: hiring and training of waitstaff, runners, bussers, hosts. The chef and sous-chef were training cooks and prep people. The menu was being created, and we were dealing with publicity details for opening night party plans and restaurant promotion in addition to dealing with contractors and construction workers who were completing the building of the restaurant in time to open. It was a roller-coaster ride.

At the eight-in-the-morning meeting, the management team was gathered for our daily briefing in my office in the two-bedroom suite on the top floor of the Dylan Hotel. There was a knock on the door, and in walked Jamie Spears, Britney's father, with two people. Jamie was stoned out of his mind. He stumbled into the room and disrupted the meeting. Up to then, Jamie had nothing to do with the restaurant, no involvement at all. From time to time, he would show up in the restaurant to see how things were coming along, so it was shocking that he would show up at a meeting and demand that I hire the couple he was with as general managers, fire the chef, hire a new chef, and change the menu.

I was doing my best to reason with Jamie to no avail. Fortunately, the young couple, after I explained the situation to them, realized that there would be no job for them. They left, understanding that Jamie had sold them a bill of goods because he was Britney's father.

But I was now left with an out-of-control drunk and a management staff shaken and insecure about their future at Nyla.

After the couple left, Jamie began screaming and knocking things off the table and threatening me physically—all in front of my staff. I managed to get him to another room and tried to talk him down and thought at any moment he would throw a punch at me. Fortunately, he ran out of steam. I got him to leave but not before he yelled, "You ain't seen the last of me yet. I'm pulling Britney out of the deal unless I get my chef and a new menu."

Hours later, I got the staff to realize that Jamie was blowing steam and assured them that I would address Jamie's outrageous behavior and that it would not happen again. And their jobs were secure, and the opening of the restaurant would happen as planned. What a way to start the day.

I called Larry Rudolph, Britney's manager, after Jamie left. He got Britney's mother on a conference call. I explained what had happened. After hearing me out, Lynne said she would take care of the problem, and she certainly did. She must have read Jamie the riot act, because the next morning, at the eight-o'clock managers' meeting, a sheepish, sober Jamie Spears walked in the office and apologized for his behavior and said that he would never again interfere with the operation of Nyla and acknowledged that Bobby is in full charge.

Everyone was relieved. I walked outside of the office with Jamie and thanked him. He promised he would not be a problem ever again. Then he asked me a favor. "Can you make sure to have Bud Light in the restaurant?"

Smiling, I told him that I liked Bud Light too and went back to work. *What's next?*

'Choices' Makes a Bad
Choice Hiring Lizzie

S ometime after my travails with the Podolsky brothers at Spread,
I was contacted by the owner of a Korean restaurant on the corner of Park Avenue South and Eighteenth Street. He told me his
restaurant was failing, and he wanted to hire me as a consultant to
turn his Koreatown restaurant around. I accepted with the understanding that the existing restaurant couldn't be salvaged and a new
one needed to be created. We agreed to my having full control of the
project, and he would approve budgets for closing and reopening
operating expenses.

I was back to my specialty: starting a project by closing a failing
restaurant, designing a new one, and taking the usual steps of getting
interior renovation, creating a new menu, hiring staff, a chef, kitchen
help, managers. The menu would be similar to Spread's, a grazing
menu with the guest selecting several appetizers as an entrée, and the
restaurant name would be Choices.

And back to Bernie Bennett doing publicity for my new restaurant venture. However, with Bernie gone, I needed a new publicist,
and Lizzie Grubman was the hot publicist in the city. She was cred-
ited with launching several successful restaurants. *New York* magazine
did a feature on her, and she became the *it* girl in the city.

I knew Lizzie from the times when her father would bring her
to Mulholland Drive Café for dinner. They were hoping she would
meet Patrick Swayze. Her father, Allen Grubman, was a well-known
theatrical attorney, and his connections gave Lizzie access to celeb-

rities who would hire her to put their restaurants and clubs on the map. I hired Lizzie for Choices.

We had a successful opening. Things were going along well. The owner was pleased with the changes I'd made. What I didn't know was that Lizzie, behind my back, was bad-mouthing me to the owner and encouraging him to replace me with her boyfriend, who would run the restaurant at half of my fee. This change would also benefit Lizzie, who was supporting her boyfriend.

After the changeover, Lizzie was involved in a notorious incident when, in a rage of anger, she backed her car into a group of people outside a Hamptons club. *What's next*

Ice-T

I first met Ice-T, the actor who was starring in the long-running TV show *Law & Order*, sometime in the early '00s. He was interested in opening a supper club, and a mutual friend of ours hooked us up, thinking that I would be a perfect partner with Ice-T in this venture. After meeting with Ice-T, we agreed we would make a good team, I with my experience in operating restaurants and Ice-T with his celebrity.

Soon after, we found a club in Greenwich Village that was for sale that we both agreed could work. We spent several months negotiating with the owner. I can't remember the details, but we didn't make a deal. However, Ice-T and I hit it off. I spent time with Ice-T and Coco, his girlfriend at the time; they have since married.

Ice-T was very charming and open to telling stories about his past. One night, over drinks, he told me that he was a bank robber when he was a young man. He would walk into a bank with a gun, stand in the middle of the bank, raise the gun in the air so everyone would see it, and announce in a very loud voice, "This is a takeover."

Why a takeover and not a bank robbery, you ask? He told me he would get a rush so exhilarating every time he would stick up a bank and got a reputation in his neighborhood as having nerves of steel. Thus, the name Ice-T took hold. He took pride in telling me it took a certain kind of person to take over a bank that even when a tough drug dealer asked to go along with him on a bank job, the drug dealer would panic and run away before going into the bank. It was fun hanging with Ice-T back then, even though we couldn't put a deal together.

Exit New York and Going South, Really South

With the bad taste of doing business with Lizzie Grubman, the Podolsky brothers, and Morris Moinian behind me, I was happy to accept an offer from a Florida-based group to run their restaurant in Aventura in North Miami. I would be a consultant. They wanted me to preopen, open, and get the place up and running. Once the owners were satisfied with the operation, my contract was over. It took six months to complete the opening of an upscale Prezzo restaurant.

Then a friend introduced me to three men who owned an Italian restaurant in Boca Raton, which they had opened less than six months earlier. There were problems, and they needed professional hands-on help. Same old story: three guys with no restaurant experience open a restaurant. I met with them: Albie Kula, Adam Kula, and Lewis Kasman. Adam was Albie's son. Kasman was Albie's son-in-law. Kasman, called "Matzo Boy" and known as John Gotti's godson, did jail time for not testifying against John Gotti.

The Kulas and Kasman were in the trimware business in New York's garment center. After Kasman got out of jail and Albie and Adam closed down their trimware business, they decided to go into the restaurant business in Boca Raton. Kasman and Adam each bought houses in the Boca area and moved their families there from Long Island. They banked on the restaurant, which they named Campagnola, to support their respective lifestyles.

After meeting with them at Campagnola, I realized that not one of them had any knowledge, background, or ability to operate a restaurant. The maître d' they hired was expected to run the restaurant. I agreed to come in as a consultant at 1,500 dollars a week and spent several weeks at the restaurant, assessing the situation and reporting back with my recommendations: food and drinks were priced too high, management was bad—so was word of mouth.

The restaurant was losing money every week. I met the Kulas and Kasman and told them that Campagnola was too far gone to be saved. They would have to close it and create a new restaurant or sell, cut their losses and move on.

The Kulas were willing to put in more money and build a new restaurant. Kasman voted to sell. He had a buyer lined up. They decided to sell and asked me to stay on to keep an eye on things until the deal was done, same 1,500-dollars-a-week fee. Each week, Adam gave me a 1,500-dollar check, and each time, he asked me not to cash it until the restaurant sold when there would be enough money in the account to cover the checks. I agreed.

While I thought Albie and Adam were honorable, I wasn't so sure about Kasman. When the restaurant sold, I was holding four checks totaling six thousand dollars. When I got to the bank to cash them, the account was closed. Albie and Adam Kula went back to Long Island. Kasman had a home in Boca, and Adam was in the process of selling his Long Island home. I tried calling Kasman. He wasn't answering. Albie and Adam were also ducking my calls.

I headed back to New York and left a message for Adam that he had to make good on the checks. "You're the one who signed them, and you're the one who gave them to me, and I'm holding you responsible, not Albie or Kasman. And if I have to, I will go to the attorney general."

He called back immediately, apologized profusely, and promised the entire six thousand dollars, one at a time—one 1,500-dollar check a week for the next four weeks. I agreed. We planned to meet at a diner in Long Island. I showed up. Adam came with his father, who gave me 1,500 dollars in cash, and I returned the check originally given to me. Then Albie asked me for the three other checks. "Sure," I said. "Give me 4,500 dollars, and they're yours."

"You don't trust us?" he queried. "We'll give you 1,500 dollars a week for the next three weeks."

"Albie, here's how it works," I told him. "You give me the 4,500 dollars, and then I give you the checks."

So the next three weeks, I drove out to the diner and collected 1,500 dollars cash each week, and each week I returned the original 1,500-dollar check given to me.

After collecting the last check, Adam called me. He knew a restaurant that was for sale in Boca Raton, and he wanted to buy it. Unbelievable. The guy knows nothing about operating a restaurant. He just took a loss on one, and now he wants to buy a restaurant. What a glutton for punishment. "Good luck," I said.

He then wanted to know if I'd like to go partners with him in this new venture. Thanks, but no thanks, and I continued, "If you are serious about buying this restaurant, I could help you as a consultant."

He liked the idea. We signed a one-year consultant manager contract for Flakowitz in Boca Raton, which was a New York-style deli known for its bagels. The ownership deal for Flakowitz was between Adam and his father Albie with Robert Pirozzi, who owned Flakowitz. The purchase price was one million dollars with a five-hundred-thousand-dollar down and five hundred thousand dollars to be paid over the next ten years. I was back in my milieu, closing, renovating, rehiring, retraining a new restaurant.

After a great start and the restaurant doing 1.5 million dollars a year and showing a modest profit, I knew the space was not being properly utilized. Seating capacity had to be increased from sixty to one hundred seats, which meant adding booths and a counter as well as capitalizing on the dinner market. Flakowitz was open from seven in the morning to three in the afternoon. In season, it was open for dinner until 8:00 p.m.

After making the changes, sales went from 1.5 million dollars to 2.2 million dollars. My deal with Adam was that I got one thousand dollars a week plus ten percent of any monthly increase over 125,000 dollars, which came to an additional five thousand dollars a month. Adam and Albie were happy with what I accomplished, and I loved making ten thousand dollars a month and living in Highland Beach on the ocean, a five-minute drive to the restaurant and a block from the office. Truthfully, I was more like the owner, and Adam, whom I took under my wing, was more like the manager.

This didn't last very long. After about eight months, Adam and Albie wanted to change our financial arrangement. They thought paying me ten percent of the increased sales was over-the-top. Rather than leave, I took the new deal. I was having too good a life to walk away. At the end of the year, when our agreement was up, Adam asked me to stay on as a consultant-manager under the changed financial terms. That deal lasted ten years.

Things were going well in the first year. After that, there was no controlling Adam. He began using the restaurant as his personal ATM. He didn't pay suppliers or sales or payroll taxes. He fell behind on payroll. He wasn't paying Robert Pirozzi's note. Didn't he get that Pirozzi could take back the restaurant on default of payment? Apparently not.

Things got dicey. I became a buffer and juggler. I was keeping the restaurant going and Pirozzi from shutting the place down for not paying taxes. Every summer, when business slowed down, I'd call Albie for an infusion of money. For years, he put in around one hundred thousand dollars. Sometimes, I had to loan Adam money so he could keep the restaurant open. When the season started and sales improved, I made certain to get my money.

At one point, I proposed taking full control of the restaurant. It was behind in taxes, in the mortgage to Pirozzi, and around two hundred thousand dollars was owed to suppliers. I'd make sure the mortgage and taxes got paid and would reduce the accounts payable to suppliers. I'd give Adam and Albie five thousand dollars a month until the end of the lease. That was my proposal.

We were in a diner in Boca. Albie was sitting next to Adam across from me. He asked me how was I going to pay everybody and give them five thousand dollars a month. What's going to be different? "Simple," I said. "You take Adam home with you to Long Island and keep him away from the restaurant."

Adam didn't like hearing that, but he didn't say anything. They didn't take the lifeline.

Before long, Pirozzi took back the restaurant. Pirozzi knew how to operate a restaurant and didn't need me. Even with plenty of time on my hands, I couldn't break one hundred playing golf. So time for *what's next*

Shit Happens, Really Happens

Shirley, the bookkeeper who worked at Flakowitz when I was there, lived in Century Village, a retirement community in Deerfield Beach, for people over fifty-five. Knowing that I was available, she told me that the only place to eat in Century Village had closed. It was a small freestanding shack between the ninth and tenth hole of the golf course and that the management of Century Village was looking for a restaurant operator to run a restaurant in that space. Shirley gave me the contact information, and I made an appointment to meet the manager and look at the restaurant.

The manager was a woman from Georgia named Kim Whitmore. Kim greeted me at the closed restaurant and showed me an empty building with a small kitchen space with no equipment. She asked me about my restaurant experience and background. I told her about my running Flakowitz in Boca, which had been there for around twenty years. There was also a Flakowitz in Boynton Beach.

Kim seemed not to know Flakowitz. She asked me what was on the menu. I explained it was a New York-style restaurant known for huge pastrami sandwiches. She asked, "What's a pastrami?" I laughed, thinking she was kidding, but she also asked if there could be tacos on the Century Village menu. I realized there was no deal here.

Curious, I asked Kim what the terms of the deal were. She said that if I was approved by the board, I would get a one-year lease and build a restaurant. In disbelief, I said, "Let me get this straight. You expect me to take an empty building and invest upwards of five

189

hundred thousand dollars to build a restaurant with a one-year lease? And what happens after the first year?"

With a straight face, she said, "Well, if we like you, you get another one-year lease."

I say, "No businessman in their right mind would take such a deal, and if you find someone willing to invest five hundred thousand dollars on a one-year term, have them committed immediately. Kim, have a nice day. I'm out of here," all said in one breath.

The next day, Kim called and said that she told the board members about me and our meeting. They insisted she get back in touch and have me come back to meet with the board. All seven members of the board knew my reputation as a restaurant operator and loved the idea of having a Flakowitz-style restaurant in Century Village. Without tacos, I hoped.

Reluctantly, I met with the board members. Knowing that I wasn't interested in making a deal and that the board members were chomping at the bit to have a Flakowitz-type restaurant in their community, I made over-the-top demands: a five-year lease and five-year option, financing of the build-out, furnishing and paying for equipment and all start-up costs, no rent. And after day-to-day expenses were paid, any profits would be mine. They agreed.

While it was too good a deal to pass up, I had misgivings. I called Robert Pirozzi and offered him the deal. In return, I wanted twenty-five percent of the business without having to be there day-to-day to run the operation. He agreed that the deal was too good to pass up, but he had just signed a lease to build a Flakowitz in Wellington, Florida, and the timing was bad for him. So now I would be the owner of a restaurant to be built and opened in Century Village, Deerfield Beach.

I began designing a one-hundred-seat restaurant with an additional twenty seats in an outside café. There would be a prep kitchen and an exposed kitchen opening to the dining room. The board approved the plans. It was then up to Century Village's manager Kim Whitmore to secure the licenses required to open the restaurant. The restaurant would be called The Clubhouse Diner and feature a Flakowitz-style menu.

Since my only overhead was food costs, labor, and some incidentals, I decided to reduce the menu prices by ten percent, making it a bargain for the Century Village residents. The build-out process took about six months to complete. The committee members decided that since opening was close to the Jewish holiday Rosh Hashanah, the first meal the restaurant served would be a traditional Rosh Hashanah dinner, and the restaurant would open the next day. It went very well, and the word of mouth was that Century Village finally had a first-class restaurant.

The next morning, as the staff was preparing to open, Deerfield Beach Building Department agents showed up at the restaurant, advising that we did not have the proper certificate of occupancy, because the building was not zoned to operate as a restaurant and couldn't open until the zoning was changed—a major, major problem.

Kim, who didn't know about pastrami, also didn't know about building permits or how long it would take to straighten everything out. Here I was with a full staff that I had been training for over a month and paying out of my own pocket, same for food and other expenses to get ready to open. I had to lay them off until everything was resolved, and they could return to work. They were not happy.

Wilbur, my main chef and cook, was the only one I kept on. He had been working at Flakowitz, and with Robert Pirozzi's approval, he left to work for me. I explained to Wilbur that I would pay him until we reopened. Unfortunately, I was relying on Kim's telling me it would take two weeks to get everything done. However, two weeks became four weeks, and four weeks became a year before The Clubhouse Diner was able and ready to open.

During that year, I lost staff and had to hire and train new staff and pay Wilbur a thousand dollars a week not to work. Worst of it all was that food costs had skyrocketed, and prices of everything went out of control. There was no way I could keep menu prices as low as I had intended a year earlier. Besides, board approval was required before menu prices could be raised.

To add to the misery, the board had just run a full-page ad showing the original menu with prices, so raising prices would cause an uprising from the eighteen thousand Century Village residents.

The board asked me to keep the prices as announced and to increase them the first of the year. That meant I would have to suffer losses from an October opening to January first, when the season began. For three months, people were lined up, waiting for a table. I was getting killed. It would be better to pay them to eat somewhere else.

When January first finally arrived and menu prices were significantly increased, there was major backlash. The residents accused me of pulling a bait and switch. Most stopped coming. The co-op board didn't allow advertising outside Century Village, and maybe worst of all, the season ended in March, and eighty percent of the residents left for the summer. It was a complete disaster. I lost a ton of money and was heading into the worst six-month business period.

Sometime in July, I threw in the towel, took my losses, and cut out. The deal that was a no-brainer—an offer I couldn't refuse—turned into an offer I should have refused. How was I to know? Shit happened. If I could know the future, I'd be back at the racetrack.

After that fiasco, I had several short-lived jobs. Michael Dezer, the man who owned the building where I opened Twenty Twenty with Ashford & Simpson twenty years earlier, now owned the Trump International Resort in Sunny Isles Beach, Florida. Dezer needed help with his restaurants in the hotel. We came to an agreement, and I spent about seven months working there.

The hotel and one of the restaurants were right on the beach. It was more like a vacation for me than it was working, just what I needed after the stress of Century Village. When that ended, I worked with restaurant owners at Blue Moon Mexican Cafe, their newly built restaurant in Boca Raton. It was beyond help and closed nine months later. I returned to New York, where I continue to contemplate my future. *What's next?*

Stay Tuned

s I sit in my Upper East Side apartment with pen to paper and
writing my memories and life experience, I realize that through
my ups and downs. I have no complaints, no significant regrets. I've
always enjoyed myself and had a good time. I'm optimistic by nature
and believe there's more to come, always checking out "what's next"
and keep reminding myself that life comes full circle. So here's to
what's next?

Menus

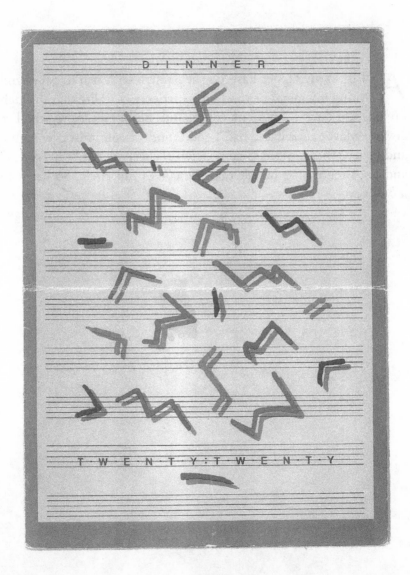

A new vision in American Regional Cooking.

STARTERS

Oysters Rockefeller $6.50
Fresh oysters baked with a parsley, spinach and scallion topping.

Fried Quahog Clams, Squibnocket Chilli Sauce $5.50
Crisp-fried tender clams with a spicy tomato chutney for dipping.

Delaware Crabcakes with Sweet Mustard Dip $7.50
Pancakes of crabmeat and lobster mousse with a light honey-mustard sauce.

Smoked Trout and Chile Torta $5.00
A chilled "pate" of smoked trout and roasted chiles, with grilled tomato salsa.

Shrimp Cocktail $7.50
Our interpretation of this American classic.

Maple Barbecued Spareribs $6.50
Maple-glazed, meaty spareribs roasted with a piquant barbecue marinade.

Angel on Horseback $14.00
Fresh duck foie gras wrapped with Amana bacon and roasted.

Today's Soup $3.50

SALADS

Crab and Lobster Louis $17.00
Crabmeat, lobster and avocado in a rich Louis dressing.

Texas BBQ-Chef's Salad $11.00
Slow-cooked BBQ brisket, turkey, smoked cheeses and greens in a light tomato-cilantro dressing.

Crackling Peanut Salad $8.00
Southern-style greens with roasted peanuts and cracklings in a sweet 'n sour traditional dressing.

Twenty-Twenty House Salad $4.50

FISH & SEAFOOD

Baked Devilled Lobster $22.00
A live lobster split, stuffed with a traditional bread & pepper mixture, buttered and roasted.

Sweetbread & Oyster Pie $18.50
A savory pie of fresh oysters and sweetbreads with wild mushrooms and summer vegetables.

Crisped Shrimp and Plantains $17.00
Tender Gulf shrimp quickly sautéed with ripe plantains.

Grilled Spiced Swordfish Steak $17.50
Grilled with an old-fashioned clove, ginger and orange marinade.

Roast, Stuffed Whole Baby Coho Salmon $16.50
A whole boned baby Salmon stuffed with wild rice and walnuts, served with a scotch whiskey cream.

Daily Fresh Fish Specials   market

MEAT, GAME AND POULTRY

Duck & Sausage Etouffée $17.00
Roast duckling and Andouille sausage smothered in a rich Creole gravy.

Panhandle-style Barbecued Quail $18.50
Boned whole quail and their giblets braised in a rich, sweet barbecue sauce then grilled.

Low Country Stuffed Fried Chicken with Cream Gravy $13.50
Pan-fried chicken stuffed with its liver and bacon.

Panéed Chicken Filet with Noodles $12.50
Crumbed and butter-sauteed chicken breast with egg noodles in bell pepper sauce.

Grilled Indiana Veal Chop with Spicy Corn Relish $21.00
Tender grilled milk-fed veal chop with fresh corn relish.

Steak 'n Beans $20.50
Grilled dry-aged prime shell steak with chili beans on the side.

Mulholland Drive Cafe

June 1988

July 27, 1988

DINNER MENU

SOUPS AND SALADS

Soup of the Day $3.00
Mixed Greens $3.50
Spinach, Bacon and Mushroom $4.50
Tomato and Mozzarella $4.50
California Spa Salad $8.50
Warm Chicken Salad $9.50
Shrimp Salad $14.50
Chef Salad $9.50

PASTAS

Individual Pizza $8.50
Pasta of the Day $8.50
Seafood Lasagna $14.50

CHICKEN

Roasted Baby Chicken $9.50
Chicken Pot Pie $9.50
Fried Chicken Samantha $10.50

SEAFOOD AND FISH

Broiled Filet of Sole $12.50
Grilled Swordfish $14.50
Grilled Salmon Steak $14.50
Sauteed Crabcakes $11.50
Seafood and Chicken Gumbo $14.50
Seafood Brochette $14.50
Shrimp with Garlic Butter $14.50
Fried Flounder $12.50

STEAKS AND CHOPS

Broiled Chopped Sirloin Steak $8.50
Sauteed Calf's Liver with Bacon and Onions $11.50
Grilled Pork Chops smothered with Puffed Shallots and Apples $10.50
Aged Sirloin Shell Steak $19.50
Hamburger $5.50

SIDES

Garlic Mashed Potato $3.50
Homemade French Fried Potato $2.50
Fried Zucchini Strips $3.50
Vegetable of the Day $3.50

DINNER

OPENING ROUND

Mixed Greens
Sliced: Tomatoes, Onions
Pickled Herring
Sour: Tomatoes, Pickles   No Charge
Cole Slaw   With Entree
Celery, Carrots and Olives
Cucumber Salad

DRESSINGS
Blue Cheese
Russian
Creamy Italian

WARM-UP

Onion Soup	$ 2.50
Soup of the Day	2.25

CLASSIC WINNERS

Ground Sirloin Steak	8.95
Roast Prime Ribs of Beef	13.50
Broiled Chicken	8.95
Barbecued Spare Ribs	10.75
Calves Liver	10.75
Lamb Chops	12.25
Veal Chop	12.75
16 oz. Prime Sirloin Steak	14.50
Filet Mignon	13.75

FRESH BROILED

Filet of Sole	8.95
Scallops	9.75
Swordfish Steak	12.75
Red Snapper	12.25
Salmon Steak	12.25

DOUBLES

Lobster Tails	14.50

MIXED DOUBLES

Lobster Tail & Filet Mignon	14.50
Barbecued Chicken & Ribs	9.50

TIE BREAKERS

Baked Potato	$ 2.50
Potato Skins	2.50
Steak Fries	2.50
Onion Rings	2.50
Sauteed Mushrooms	2.50
Fried Zucchini	2.50
Fried Cauliflower	2.50
Vegetable of the Day	2.50

FINALS

Stuffed Ice Cream	2.75
Cheese Cake	3.00
Chocolate Mousse Cake	3.50
Carrot Cake	2.75
Pecan Pie	2.75
Chocolate/Chocolate Chip Cake	3.00
Apple Pie	2.75
Strawberry Shortcake	3.00
Delice Triple Mousse Cake	3.75
Fresh Strawberries with Fresh Whip Cream	3.50
Fresh Fruit Cup	2.75
Melon in Season	2.50

LATE ENTRIES
Served After 8:00 P.M.

SALADS

Salad Bar	5.95
Nicoise	6.95
Chef	6.95
Chicken Waldorf	6.95

OMELETTES

Caviar, Onion, Sour Cream	6.50
Apple and Sausage	5.75
Lox, Eggs & Onions	5.95
Choice	4.95

SPECIALTIES

Hamburger with Steak Fries or Onion Rings	4.95
12 oz. Prime Sirloin Steak with Fries	10.95
Quiche Lorraine with Tossed Salad	5.75
Nova Platter with Bagel	6.50
Reuben Sandwich	5.95
Club Sandwich	5.95
(Salad Bar not included with Late Entries)	

Articles & Recipes by Bobby

A Reformed Restaurateur Reviews Restaurant Reviewers

By Bobby Ochs
Published 10 Nov 2021 in 'Our Town'
The local paper for the Upper East Side

I always believed a judge should have to serve three months in prison before being admitted to the bench and able to sentence anyone to prison time. I feel the same way about restaurant reviewers. In my opinion, a restaurant reviewer must have a serious financial investment and at least one year of actively operating a restaurant before being allowed to write a restaurant review. (Although for some reviewers one year in prison would work just fine.) Since the pandemic, the NY Times continues writing about restaurants but hasn't been giving star ratings.

As a long time NYC restaurateur, I've had my share of good and not-so-good reviews and understand the concept of public service in letting the public know the pros and cons and ups and downs of a restaurant's food, atmosphere, service. However, someone will have to explain to me the importance or the value of a reviewer's commenting on the attire of an owner. Me, for instance. Back in 1985, when I was opening Twenty Twenty with Ashford & Simpson, a reviewer from a hip downtown magazine, critiqued my dinner jacket as "absolutely hideous." Really, what does my taste in what I wear have anything to do with reviewing a restaurant?

Lucky that reviewer wasn't on the beat in 1981 when one night the chef at Marigold, a restaurant I owned on Madison Ave., forgot to put the chicken in the Chicken Pot Pie. Now that deserved a slam. The chef forgot. Somehow forgot the eponymous ingredient in the dish. Not easy, I'm sure, but he did. I found out about the missing chicken from several guests. And you can be sure there was a chicken in every pot ever after. Marigold went on to be successful for the 10-year length of its lease and Chicken Pot Pie was a menu favorite to the very end.

In the 90s, when I owned Mulholland Drive Café with Patrick Swayze, I was invited to be on the John McLauglin Show, along with Elaine Kaufman who owned Elaine's, Barbara Smith who owned B. Smith's, and Tim Zagat who published Zagat's restaurant review guide. After an hour of John McLauglin's asking each of us about the details of opening and operating a successful restaurant, it was clear to me, Elaine, and Barbara that Zagat had no idea of the internal workings of a restaurant and that Zagat, a lawyer, whose experience with restaurants was apparently dining in them.

After that, I instructed my publicist Bernie Bennett to keep all restaurant reviewers away from Mulholland Drive Café. A publicist generally was hired to get a restaurant reviewed. With Mullholland Drive Café, that wasn't really necessary. The place was always busy for lunch and dinner. At dinner people were waiting almost an hour for a seat at one of the 170 seats or 30 bar seats. There was no need to be reviewed by a so-called reviewer, maybe maven. As a restaurateur, nothing beats a mention of your restaurant in a Cindy Adams or Page Six column.

Favorite Review

Through all the years of owning restaurants, and the many reviewers reviewing them, my favorite review was by Thea Sands of this very newspaper. I remember her well-written review of Samantha Restaurant back in 1978. She noted the excellent service, the delicious lemony hollandaise sauce on the eggs benedict at Sunday Brunch, and the well-run restaurant. At the end of the day, the best review is the old-fashioned word of mouth you get from satisfied guests who come to your restaurant because they enjoy the food and service and environment and are treated well. They tell their friends who tell their friends. Sound old fashioned? Too good to be true? I don't think so.

Now that I'm out of the restaurant business and don't have to worry about reviewers and the day-to-day operation of running a restaurant, I find enjoyment in my weekly trip to Costco with my wife Carolyn and our downstairs neighbors, Michael and Barbara Kurzman. Before the weekly drive, I make a menu for each night's dinner that I'll be cooking for my family. Cooking for three is a lot less stressful than cooking 300 dinners a night even if the chef's doing the cooking. I do it all with a chef's mise en place in front of me—the makings of a large martini—and then start on the meatballs and the sauce for my Meatballs and Spaghetti specialty which has been well reviewed by my wife Carolyn and my daughter Samantha who Instagrams the meal to her followers, letting them know of her dad's culinary talents. And there's high praise from the Kurzmans whose dinner is delivered to their door. Personally, by me, a reformed restaurateur.

When New York Was a Restaurant Town

By Bobby Ochs
Published 17 Mar 2021 in 'Our Town'
The local paper for the Upper East Side

I'm a born and bred New Yorker. I've lived with my wife Carolyn on the UES for more than 55 years. Pandemic, no pandemic, taxes, no taxes, I'm here to stay. Professionally, I've been a restaurateur and have owned restaurants with celebrity partners and others who weren't. Before owning restaurants, I worked in them. Restaurants are my life. In my DNA. These days I neither work in nor own a restaurant. When I walk around today's New York, I'm overwhelmed with memories of when NY was a restaurant town.

The restaurant industry has certainly changed from my days in the business starting in the 70's and continuing through the early aughts. Today, the pandemic has forced restaurant owners to take drastic steps to stay in business—serving food and drinks outside on the street in freezing weather, changing limits of occupancy, building outdoor structures, paying Grubhub, Uber Eats, Door Dash, et al for delivery to hungry New Yorkers grounded in their apartments. And, for better or worse, this is the likely direction of New York restaurants.

Back in my day, restaurants, bars, and night clubs were the life-line of the city. New Yorkers went to restaurants before and after a day or evening activity or event. They socialized at restaurants for entertainment. If you had tickets to a B'way show, it was Sardi's or Joe Allen's or Rosoff's. If you were going to see the Knicks play or to see some of the greatest college basketball teams in the country at the old Madison Square Garden (between 49th and 50th on Eighth Ave.), you sat down for a pastrami sandwich and a potato knish at the Carnegie Deli. In 1968 when the Garden moved to 32nd and Eighth Ave/, Al Cooper's on 36th St. in the heart of the Garment Center, was where you went for dinner and cocktails.

For those who hit the track and had a good night at Yonkers Raceway, it was dinner and drinks at Dominick's on Arthur Ave in the Bronx where they had the best veal parmigiana in the city. Or to the Lobster Box on City Island for a steamed lobster. On the nights that things didn't go well at the track, you headed for Dewey Wong's where Dewey would extend credit for the best shrimp and black bean sauce with fried rice. Who needed Netflix and TV when you could see Sammy Davis Jr. live at the Copa, Tony Bennett at Basin Street East, Steve (Lawrence) and Edie (Gorme) at the Empire Room in the Waldorf? Or a young Woody Allen at the Blue Angel?

I remember seeing Joan Rivers and Rodney Dangerfield as new-comers at Upstairs at the Duplex in the Village. At 4 in the morning, after an evening at one of those night clubs, we would head up to Harlem to the original Patsy's on First Ave. and 116th St. for drinks and a bowl of pasta fagiola. Or head down to Chinatown to 69 Mott for spare ribs and a huge lobster roll. And there was always the Brasserie at 4 a.m. for the largest apple pancake you ever ate. I loved seeing Baryshnikov dance at Lincoln Center followed by a burger and a beer either at O'Neals' or the Ginger Man.

Then there was the First Ave. scene for a night of bar hopping, meeting new friends and getting together with old ones. You could start at Skitch Henderson's Daly's Daffodil, move on to TGI Friday's, then to Warner Leroy's Maxwell's Plum. You never knew who you would see there. Mr. Laff's, right next door, was where Yankee short-stop Phil Linz held court nightly. Then, making your way north on First Ave. you could stop at Jerry Brodie's Muggs for one of the twenty varieties of burgers on the menu and wash it down with an ice cold beer on tap.

Maybe after hitting a few more spots you could end the night at Elaine's where the literary crowd gathered. You could always count on Elaine to be there to show you to the bar or a table with some sort of wisecrack. Things didn't slow down on Sundays. For some restaurants, it even picked up with brunch. One of my restaurants, Samantha's at First Ave. and 78th St., offered the best bang for your buck brunch. Bloody Mary, fresh fruit cup, eggs benedict and coffee for $3.95. Upper East Siders lined up every Sunday from 11 a.m. til 4 p.m.

Those days are history and so are the city's restaurants I knew. I'd like to give a special nod to some of the old favorites spots I would frequent. Bruno's on East 58th St., where Izzy Snow, a bookie from my Bronx boyhood, would buy dinner for all of his clients every Wednesday and Friday night and then lead us up to the second floor for an all night crap game...Il Vagabondo for Italian food and a game of bocci...Michael's Pub, where Gil Wiest made sure the food and live music was always great and that he had a weekly ad in local papers promoting Woody Allen's band...Jim McMullen's comfortable UES hangout...Rick Newman's Catch a Rising Star for a fun night...the Red Tulip for a classic chicken paprikash. And who could forget Sign of the Dove for a romantic dinner, where the maitre d' would present a woman with a menu without prices and the man with a menu with the pricey prices. Quaint, maybe clever, but would never happen today.

As for me, I gained fame and celebrity in the restaurant world by partnering with celebrities—Patrick Swayze at Mulholland Drive Cafe. Marla Maples at Peaches. Britney Spears at Nyla. Ashford and Simpson (Nick and Valerie) at Twenty Twenty. I learned early on, when I owned my first restaurant, that people loved going to restaurants where celebrities went. And Samantha's, named for my daughter Samantha and which I owned with two non-celebrities, was a block away from Rick Newman's Catch a Rising Star. Young and up and coming talents like Robin Williams, Pat Benatar, Rodney Dangerfield, Andy "Latke" Kaufman performed there and ended the night at Samantha's for dinner and drinks. When word got out, Samantha's was packed. I was on my way to find a celebrity to partner with in a restaurant. It worked. Those were the days.

A Restaurateur's Recipes for the Holidays

Revisiting Samantha's Chicken Tetrazzini and
Mulholland Drive Cafe's Garlic Mashed Potatoes
By Bobby Ochs
Published 10 Dec 2021 in 'Our Town'
The local paper for the Upper East Side

I've owned and operated many different restaurants for over 55 years starting back in 1960, when a hamburger and French fries were on the menu for $1.50 at the Stadium Lounge in the Bronx. I've handled all aspects of running restaurants—from bartending at Conrad's Cloud Room to flipping burgers at Arnie Rosen's Farnie's Second Avenue Steak Parlour when the cook had one too many (and I don't mean burgers)—to washing dishes at my own restaurants when a dishwasher didn't show up. I've even stood in for the chef when he didn't show.

So over the many years and the many restaurants I've worked in or owned, I've managed to accumulate a large collection of recipes, mostly by eating at other restaurants, exploring and creating menus, reading cookbooks and collaborating with the chefs when it came time to order ingredients. Sometimes I'd write down the recipes, but I'd always commit them to memory and, in the days before the celebrity chef, I knew that I couldn't open an upscale full-service restaurant unless the menu was creative and au courant. I'd read cookbooks, newspapers (no Google in those days) and watch chefs prepare dishes.

In 1978, when I was opening Samantha, the first restaurant I owned, I made the menu before hiring a chef. That's how I did it for all my restaurants. One of the first entrees at Samantha was Chicken Tetrazzini. It was a tasty, attractive dish, and diners could take their leftovers home in a doggy bag. It was a menu staple and a great dish at holiday time. (Historical note: back in the 70s and maybe early 80s, doggy bags weren't in fashion. Diners would whisper that they'd like "something" to put the leftovers in to take home for their dog.

Usually they didn't have a dog and, if they did, the dog wasn't getting the leftovers. They were. So the doggy bag was born.)

Chicken Tetrazzini serves 10 to 12 people, or enough to serve a family of 4 for three nights. Before starting, I set out the ingredients, along with the makings of a martini for myself, which I enjoy sipping while I'm cooking. Of course, the martini is optional, but highly recommended.

Here's my rendition of Samantha's Chicken Tetrazzini recipe:

CHICKEN TETRAZZINI

Ingredients:
2 boneless & skinless chicken breasts sliced into bite-size pieces from a pre-cooked chicken (turkey can be substituted for chicken)
9 Tablespoons butter
2 Tablespoons olive oil
1 lb. sliced mushrooms
1 large onion diced
5 cloves garlic minced
1 tablespoon fresh thyme leaves chopped
1/2 cup dry white wine
1/3 cup flour
4 cups whole milk
1 cup heavy cream
1 cup chicken broth
12 oz. spaghetti
1 cup grated parmesan cheese
1/4 cup bread crumbs
3/4 cup frozen peas, thawed
8 oz. water chestnuts

Directions:
Preheat oven to 450 degrees.

Spread 1 tablespoon butter over a 9" x 13" x 2" baking dish, add chicken to dish.

Coat large frying pan with oil & 1 tablespoon butter, and over medium high heat saute mushrooms till golden pale (about 10 minutes).

Add onion, garlic, & thyme, saute til onion translucent (about 8 minutes), add wine & simmer til evaporates (about 2 minutes).

Transfer mushroom mixture in with the chicken.

Start cooking spaghetti until al dente.

Melt 3 more tablespoons butter in pan over medium-low heat, add flour and whisk about 2 minutes, then whisk in milk, heavy cream, chicken broth, salt and pepper.

Increase the heat to high cover and bring to a boil. Simmer uncovered til thickens, slightly whisking (about 10 minutes).

Add peas, water chestnuts and spaghetti to chicken and mushroom mixture. Pour cream sauce over to cover chicken mixture.

Combine Parmesan cheese and breadcrumbs and sprinkle on top of chicken mixture. Dot with 3 tablespoons butter.

Bake for about 25 minutes until golden brown and bubbles. Let sit for 10–15 minutes before serving—makes 8 very large servings

Now you know why a martini is needed to get through this recipe.

Then came Mulholland Drive Cafe, the restaurant I owned with "Dirty Dancing" star Patrick Swayze, where the signature dish on the menu was Garlic Mashed Potatoes. It was a show-stopper. As the server carried in a platter of the mile-high potatoes, usually ordered as a side dish for the entire table, every diner turned their heads and waved their hands beckoning the server to bring an order to their table. Garlic mashed potatoes are a terrific side dish for most any holiday and an easy dish to make at home.

Here's the Mulholland Drive Cafe recipe:

GARLIC MASHED POTATOES

Ingredients:
1 head garlic
Olive oil
2 lbs. russet potatoes peeled and quartered
salt and freshly ground black pepper
5 Tablespoons butter
3/4 cup heavy cream

Directions:
Preheat oven to 425 degrees.

Slice off the very top of the garlic head. Drizzle head with olive oil and wrap in tin foil. Place on a sheet tray and bake until tender about 35 minutes.

Remove from oven and let cool. Remove the cloves and mash with a spoon.

Place potatoes in a large pot and cover with cold water. Add salt and bring to a boil. Cook until fork tender and drain. Mash the potatoes until smooth.

Meanwhile, heat butter and cream until butter melts add the roasted garlic and potatoes and mash together. Taste and season with salt and pepper.

Now that I'm no longer running restaurants and am a home chef, not only do I make the menu, shop for the ingredients and follow the recipes in my mind and those I've scribbled on 3x5s, but I make them for my wife and daughter and sometimes for the Kurzmans, our downstairs neighbors. And I make sure there's a place for me at the table and enough for leftovers for a day or two.

An Ochs family favorite

MEATBALLS AND SAUSAGE

Ingredients:
1lb chop meat (80-20)
1/2 lb ground pork
6 sweet Italian sausages
2 onions diced (1 for sauce)
6 cloves garlic minced
olive oil—1 tablespoons plus 1 teaspoon dry basil
1 teaspoon dry oregano
1 teaspoon dry rosemary
1/4 cup fresh Italian flat leaf parsley finely chopped
pinch red pepper flakes
2 teaspoons kosher salt
1/2 teaspoon freshly ground black pepper
2 eggs beaten lightly
1 cup seasoned dry bread crumbs
1 cup parmesan cheese
(2) 28 oz can San Marzano peeled tomatoes
1 lb spaghetti

Directions: Heat 1 tbsp oil in skillet. Sauté 1 diced onion & the garlic until onion is translucent. Let cool. In a large bowl combine chop meat, ground pork, basil, oregano, rosemary, parsley, red pepper flakes, salt, pepper, onions, garlic, eggs, bread crumbs, parmesan cheese, and mix by hand to get a pliable texture. Shape into golf ball size meatballs. Refrigerate for 1 hour. Heat 1 tbsp olive oil in a large (12 inch) skillet. Sauté the sausages over medium heat until brown. Remove and cut into bite size pieces. In the same pan pour olive oil to a depth of 1/4 inch. Heat oil. In batches place the meatballs in the oil and brown them well on all sides over medium-low heat. Remove meatballs to a plate. For the sauce, heat 1 tbsp oil in the same pan. Add 1 diced onion and sauté over medium heat until translucent. Add 1 1/2 teasps minced garlic and 1 tbsp dry basil. Stir in and crush tomatoes. Add in meatballs and sausage cover and let simmer for 25 to 30 minutes. Serve hot on cooked al dente spaghetti. Don't forget to top with grated parmesan. Bon Appetite.

Marla's Favorite from Peaches

MARINATED LOIN OF PORK WITH PORT WINE & PEPPERCORN SAUCE

Serves 6

Ingredients: 3 lbs. boneless loin of pork, trimmed, and sliced into ¼"-thick medallions

Marinade (prepare the day before)
2 cups olive oil
1 tbsp paprika
1 tbsp dried oregano
1 tsp minced fresh parsley

Port wine and peppercorn sauce
2 tsp olive oil or unsalted butter
2 cups port wine
¼ lb shallots, peeled and sliced 1/8" thick
10 black peppercorns
1 bay leaf
1 tbsp fresh thyme leaves, or 1 tsp dried thyme
2 quarts veal stock (may be purchased at a gourmet store)
1 tbsp Worcestershire sauce
1 tbsp coarse, grainy mustard, such as Pommery

Directions: Marinade: Combine all ingredients in a large bowl or pan. Place pork medallions in marinade and refrigerate covered for 24 hours.

Sauce: Place olive oil or butter in large, heavy-duty saucepan. Add shallots and cook until dark golden brown and slightly caramelized. Add peppercorns, herbs and port wine. Cook uncovered until port is reduced until almost dry. Add veal stock and Worcestershire sauce and keep simmering until reduced by half. Strain the mixture through a fine sieve and set aside. May be made ahead of time and refrigerated or frozen.

Final preparation: Grill pork 2–3 minutes on each side, to desired temperature. In a saucepan, heat 2 cups Port Wine Peppercorn Sauce until hot. Stir in 1 tbsp mustard. Place 3–4 pork medallions on each plate. Serve with sauce and mashed potatoes with Truffle Oil.

MASHED POTATOES WITH TRUFFLE OIL

Serves 6

Ingredients:
2 ½ lbs Idaho potatoes, peeled and roughly sliced
½ cup heavy cream
4 tbsp butter
1 tsp truffle oil (available at gourmet stores)
Salt and Pepper to taste

Directions: Cover potatoes with cold water and cook until tender. Drain and mash until smooth with cream, butter, salt and pepper. Add truffle oil and mix in just before serving.

Patrick's Favorite from Mullholland Drive Café

CHICKEN POT PIE

Serves 4
Prep time: 1 hour
Cooking time: 25 minutes

Ingredients:
1 whole chicken
1 carrot, sliced thick
1 rib celery, sliced thick
1 medium onion, halved
10 cups water
1 bay leaf
¼ tsp freshly ground pepper
½ cup diced peeled carrot
½ cup diced celery
1 cup frozen pearl onions
1 red pepper, sliced
8 oz fresh mushrooms, quartered
½ cup frozen peas
3 tbsp butter or margarine
3 tbsp all purpose flour
½ cup milk
1 tsp Worcestershire sauce
½ tsp salt
Dash red pepper sauce
1 package (2 sheets) frozen puff pastry, thawed according
    to package directions
1 large egg, lightly beaten

Directions: Combine chicken, sliced carrot and celery, the onion, water, bay leaf and pepper in large pot. Bring to boil. Reduce heat to low and skim surface. Simmer, partially covered, 1 hour, turning chicken after 30 minutes. Remove chicken. Cool; strain chicken broth and remove fat. Reserve 2 cups broth.

Remove skin and bones from meat; tear into large pieces. Transfer to bowl.

Bring reserved chicken broth to boil in large saucepan. Add diced carrots and celery; reduce heat and simmer 5 minutes. Add pearl onions and red pepper; simmer 1 minute. Add mushrooms and peas; simmer 1 minute more. With slotted spoon, transfer vegetables to chicken. Reserve broth.

Melt butter in medium saucepan over medium-high heat. Add flour and cook, whisking constantly, 1 minute. Whisk in reserved chicken brother and the milk, Worcestershire, salt and pepper sauce. Simmer 5 minutes, whisking occasionally. Add to chicken and vegetables and stir to combine.

Preheat oven to 425 degrees F. Spoon chicken mixture into 4 ovenproof individual baking dishes. Cut 4 circles from pastry 2 inches larger than top of dish. Cut 1-inch hole in center of each circle for vent. Place pastry on dishes; flute edges. Brush with beaten egg.

Bake pot pies on cookie sheet until tops are golden and filling is bubbly, about 25 minutes.

Britney's favorite dish from NYLA

FRIED CHICKEN

Serves 4

Ingredients:
1 broiler/fryer chicken, cut into 8 pieces
2 cups buttermilk
2 tablespoons kosher salt
2 tablespoons paprika
2 tablespoons garlic powder
2 tablespoons onion powder
1 teaspoon cayenne pepper
3 cups all purpose flour
vegetable oil for frying

Directions: Place chicken pieces into a plastic container and cover with the buttermilk. Cover and refrigerate for 12 to 24 hours. Put about 3 inches of vegetable oil in a deep pot over high heat to 350 degrees. Combine flour, salt, paprika, onion powder, garlic powder, and cayenne pepper in a large shallow platter. Drain chicken and pat dry. Reserve buttermilk. Dredge chicken pieces in flour mixture. Then dip them into buttermilk and dredge chicken again in seasoned flour. Once the oil has reached 350 degrees, working in batches carefully place chicken pieces 3 or 4 at a time in oil, fry turning pieces once, until golden brown and cooked through, about 12 minutes. Remove and drain chicken on a rack over a sheet pan. Serve hot and enjoy.

Bobby in the News

Bobby Ochs' restaurant was the place to be in the '80s
By Cindy Adams
Published February 15, 2022 in the New York Post

The '80s. Times we actually had restaurants including Bobby Ochs' high-class eatery Mulholland Drive Cafe. Co-owner was Patrick Swayze. His hangout has gone. His memory hasn't. Comes now autobio "Bobby Ochs: Kid From The Bronx and Restaurant

Partner to the Stars—From Kasha Varnishkes to Caviar to Humble Pies." The title's longer than the menu.

His additional eatery was to be called Pinky but partner Britney Spears said: "Justin Timberlake gave that name to me. I don't want this called that. Reminds me of Justin when he was my boyfriend."

Steady customers like Jackie Mason, Gay Talese. Milk was $1.59, apples 39 cents a pound, bacon $1.69, a stomach full of macaroni 50 cents, bread 55 cents, if you hungered for broccoli—which absolutely no human on Earth does—39 cents.

Bobby's parents, Polish immigrants. First generation American, Bronx born, Bobby enlisted at 17. His orphaned father became the dental mechanic who made Leon Trotsky's false teeth. Bobby dreamed of auctioning those at Christie's, but Trotsky died with Daddy's molars still in his mouth. The kid's school ended in a basketball scandal, which it's rude to talk about.

Mid-'80s he and Ashford & Simpson co-owned a nightclub. Then came Peaches with co-owner Marla Maples. Next, the downside. Enter the tax man. Mulholland Drive went kaput. He had to unload his condo.

John Travolta has said he'd like to play Bobby in the story of his life.

About the Author

BOBBY OCHS TURNS "50"

" *Kid, I give 8 to 5 against you ever making it to 25"*
Smilin Artie; Bronx, New York; 1955

" *Listen here fella — if you ever pull that stunt again,*
I give you 3 to 2, you never make your 40th birthday"
Hymie The Turk; Bronx, New York 1962

" *Son, you better change your way of life, or you're*
a favorite not to make 50."
Detective Burke, 44th precinct; Bronx New York; 1968

" *Ochs, if you keep this up, I guarantee, you'll never see another*
birthday."
Carolyn Atlas Ochs; New York City; 1985

YOU ARE INVITED
TO CELEBRATE AND WATCH ME CASH THOSE BETS

DATE: Friday: June 12, 1992   TIME: 7:30PM

PLACE: Americas Society • 680 Park Avenue - at 68th Street

RSVP: by May 29th — Susan Lippert
(Monday to Friday 11:00AM - 5:00PM) • (212) 319-7740

DRESS: Fancy Fun

B obby Ochs' story is that of a first generation American, the youngest of four children, born in 1942, in the Bronx. His life experience mirrors the generations of the times.

At 17 years old he enlisted in the Army Reserves. While serving his six-month active duty and with his take-no-prisoners attitude at Fort Gordon, Georgia, Bobby was able to bypass the rigors of training by one-upping the brass and getting himself assigned to the cushy duty in Headquarters Company. Then came the Berlin Crisis when John F. Kennedy recalled the Army Reserves, and Bobby's outfit was sent to Fort Bragg, North Carolina. There, a brash Bobby and a barracks full of brash New York recruits wrote a Christmas show and spent the rest of their army service performing for the troops. Bobby's portrayal of a forlorn sad sack soldier pining to go home for Christmas stole the show, and the troop was featured in a four-page spread in the New York Times magazine.

In his memoir, he regales with stories of growing up, after his mother died when he was seven years old, playing pool, spending his nights at the racetrack, working as a bartender and managing restaurants. He writes about the irreverent, profligate spending of the Yuppie and Boomer years when he was a restaurateur and partner to the stars. And the consulting years when he was creating and re-creating restaurants for clients—and was always a bystander to the digital natives of the X, Y, Z and beyond Generations as a raconteur and a guy who kept asking and moved on to what's next.

Today, Bobby's out mulling the world, the scene. He's still recognized by many from the days he owned the popular Mulholland Drive Cafe with Dirty Dancing's Patrick Swayze, the David Rockwell designed Twenty-Twenty with Ashford & Simpson, Peaches with Marla Maples when she was married to Donald Trump, and Nyla with Britney Spears. Some even remember him as the restaurateur who made the Sunday brunch mimosa a happening in Manhattan when he owned his first restaurant, Samantha's, on the Upper East Side.

He tells the story of spending time in Las Vegas with a young John Travolta and his manager when Travolta, after making Saturday Night Fever, was interested in playing Bobby if a movie was made of his gambling days growing up in the Bronx. And the story of how Mullholland Drive Cafe came to be, and then was no more.

Growing up in the Bronx in the '40s and '50s, losing his mother when he was seven, Bobby found a home away from home at the neighborhood pool room from the time he was 13, and at the

Sugar Bowl, a luncheonette opposite Taft High School. The Damon Runyon characters he came in contact with in these hangouts had monikers like Smilin' Artie, Moishe the Senator, Hymie the Turk, and were his mentors. He was one of the motley crew who spent their days betting on every sport imaginable and handicapping for their nights at the racetrack.

Family was very much a part of Bobby's youth. His sisters, brother, aunts, uncles, cousins were part of his life. His dad, Adolph Ochs, was a dental mechanic with an office not too far from where they lived and had the distinction of having made Leon Trotsky's false teeth. Bobby tells how his father's love of going to the racetrack was passed on to him.

Celebrity was always waiting in the wings for Bobby Ochs from the time he was born like when his Polish immigrant parents listened to their 13-year old daughter and 18-year old niece, who wanted the new baby, if it was a boy, named Robert after the 1940's movie star heart throb, Robert Taylor. So defying the Jewish tradition of naming newborns after the dearly departed, they named their son, Robert.

These days Bobby's a home chef extraordinaire—shopping at Costco, at Leonards, re-creating retro recipes from his restaurant days, prepping them with his favorite martini mis en plas in place, and serving dinner to his wife Carolyn, his daughter Samantha, and the Kurzmans, his downstairs neighbors. And writing about his life in the restaurant world and sharing his recipes in Our Town newspaper. With an eye out for what's next.